Let it Glow!

108 Recipes for Radiance

Pratibha Masand Sachdev

Copyright © 2014 Pratibha Masand Sachdev.

All rights reserved. No part of this book may be used or reproduced by any means, graphic, electronic, or mechanical, including photocopying, recording, taping or by any information storage retrieval system without the written permission of the publisher except in the case of brief quotations embodied in critical articles and reviews.

Author Credits: MA, CHHC

Balboa Press books may be ordered through booksellers or by contacting:

Balboa Press
A Division of Hay House
1663 Liberty Drive
Bloomington, IN 47403
www.balboapress.com
1 (877) 407-4847

Because of the dynamic nature of the Internet, any web addresses or links contained in this book may have changed since publication and may no longer be valid. The views expressed in this work are solely those of the author and do not necessarily reflect the views of the publisher, and the publisher hereby disclaims any responsibility for them.

The author of this book does not dispense medical advice or prescribe the use of any technique as a form of treatment for physical, emotional, or medical problems without the advice of a physician, either directly or indirectly. The intent of the author is only to offer information of a general nature to help you in your quest for emotional and spiritual well-being. In the event you use any of the information in this book for yourself, which is your constitutional right, the author and the publisher assume no responsibility for your actions.

Any people depicted in stock imagery provided by Thinkstock are models, and such images are being used for illustrative purposes only.
Certain stock imagery © Thinkstock.

Printed in the United States of America.

ISBN: 978-1-4525-2333-0 (sc)
ISBN: 978-1-4525-2335-4 (hc)
ISBN: 978-1-4525-2334-7 (e)

Library of Congress Control Number: 2014917999

Balboa Press rev. date: 10/10/2014

Praise for *Let it Glow!*

"This delightfully heartfelt and powerfully written collection of true stories, recipes, and daily practices shows one modern Indian woman's journey through hard times using wisdom gathered from her precious grandmother and talented aunts. Bravely sharing how she personally has been able to rediscover joy, health and inner nourishment, Pratibha Masand Sachdev offers her family recipes for you to use along with your own intuition to discover what ignites your own special glow. What a beautiful gift!"
Melanie Sachs - Author
Ayurvedic Beauty Care: Ageless Techniques
to Invoke Natural Beauty

"Influenced by her Vedic ancestors, Pratibha's book Let it Glow! 108 Recipes for Radiance passionately demonstrates that each one of us has the power to heal ourselves with Mother Nature's wholesome food. Through her reputable work as a health practitioner, she presents a delicate blend of wholesome recipes based in Ayurveda's immutable principle of self-nourishment. Your health will surely be fed, feasted and blessed by this wealth of flavors."
Bri. Maya Tiwari - Author The Path of Practice

"Let it glow nourishes your body with conscious recipes and feeds your soul with one woman's journey to joy. A great guide to ignite your inner light."
Aimee DuFresne, Joy Catalyst and Author of
Keep Going: From Grief to Growth.

Vakratunda Mahaakaaya
Suryakoti Samaprabha
Nirvighnam Kurume Deva
Sarvakaaryeshhu Sarvadaa
O elephant headed and large bodied Ganesha,
Radiant as a thousand suns,
I ask for your grace
So that this task that I undertake
May complete without any hindrance

To Sugi and her children.....with love

This mind to mind
Intercourse
We have had
Your eyes piercing mine
Correcting and guiding
Holding my hand
Until
You
Saw perfection

A little mellow
I hold on to the memory
Of your weathered hands
Caressing each grain, vegetable
Spice and utensil
Chanting, singing, praying
As we cooked

Word to word
Verbal embraces
That we have shared
Have me impregnated
With ideas new and old
The gestation period
Has lasted too long

This beautiful baby
Of your ancient wisdom
And my novel awareness
Is
Ready to be delivered

These labor pains
Nourish my body, my soul
And my very being
It is not easy to
Let go of
All that I have
Nurtured so far

As this baby of our
Love for nourishing others
Comes into this
World
My book on our culinary love is complete!

table of contents....*vishaysuchi*

I.	gratitude....*abhaar*	1
II.	introduction....*parichay*	7
III.	prelude....*bhumika*	11
IV.	background....*prashthabhumi*	15
V.	introspection....*atmaparikshan*	23
VI.	regrowth....*punarviddhi*	33
VII.	nurture....*posharn*	41
VIII.	aesthetics....*saundarya*	51
IX.	deontology....*acharan rasayana*	75
X.	uplift....*utthaan*	85
XI.	food recipes....*vyanjan, samagri, seedho and vidhi*	91
XII.	skincare recipes and treatments....*nuskhe aur upchaar*	139
XIII.	conclusion....*nishkarsh*	157
XIV.	glossary....*shabdhkosh*	163
XV.	bibliography....*granthsuchi*	171

gratitude....abhaar

guru gobind dohu khare, kakey lagoon paay?
balihari guru aapne jin gobind diyo milaay!

– Kabir

On the path of self – discovery, I met my teacher and my God, I was in a dilemma, who should I bow down to first. In gratitude, I bow down to my teacher for leading me to God!

– Kabir

Life has presented me with many teachers and many lessons, from a very early age on. My journey from India to Barbados, then back to India and finally to America, which I now call my home; exposed me to many wonderful mentors. Each and every soul that crossed my path has taught me a precious lesson, either by imparting a nugget of wisdom or a morsel of bittersweet challenge. As the canvas of my life was being painted, sometimes I became the brush, sometimes the color and at other times I became the artist. I realized that the choice was always mine, to accept and surrender or to walk away. I thank the Universe for those who shaped me, polishing me with love and for the ones who grated and shaped me for the good. For every painful rub and harsh grate only allowed me to shine with grace and serve with greater love.

I offer my *saadar pranam* or respectful gratitude to my spiritual *Guru's*; *Sai, Satya and Amma* for their grace and blessings.

This book is a *shradhanjali* or a homage my paternal grandmother *Sugi Boolchand Masand*. Thanks for embracing me, nurturing me, inspiring me, and loving me; I love you.

Hardik dhanyawad or heartfelt gratitude, to all my readers who have chosen to read this book.

Thanks to my Grand Uncles, *Bhai Sahib Arjandas Masand* and *Kaviraj Kishinchand Punjabi*; for introducing me to the wonderful world of Ayurveda and the power of prayer at a very tender age. Very sick and ailing, I had returned from a long summer vacation in Haridwar, where I was diagnosed with severe jaundice. A physician trained in modern medicine, my uncle *Dr. Vishno Wadhwani* joined hands with *Dada Kishinchand* a traditional ayurvedic doctor. Together they nursed me back to good health. A beautiful marriage of ancient wisdom and modern scientific advances unfolded right in front of my eyes as I healed my body.

In gratitude to my beloved father Late *Ratanlal Masand* for inculcating me with a love of History and Herbology. My incessant queries about herbs, elements, nature, prayers, rituals or lack thereof were always answered. Sometimes they were answered with a smile and in a very playful manner and at other times with solemn seriousness. Woven into this tapestry of my life, is the love of many paternal aunts, uncles and cousins; *Sugi's* children. I would especially like to thank *Nanik, Ashok, Jawahar, Anil, Kamu* and *Omesh Masand* for their unconditional love.

Thank you, *Meera* and *Vinod Lal*, my parents for welcoming me into your life, with a gift of two loving siblings and their families. I express my gratitude also to our late grandparents, *Pesumal* and *Indira Satdev*, for blessing us always.

I am in debt to *Melanie* and *Robert Sachs*, who dusted the cobwebs off my knowledge and brought forth many time tested Ayurvedic beauty therapies for introspection and integration. Somewhere in modern day to day living, lessons learned earlier but hidden in the childhood memory resurfaced many years later. Thanks for guiding me with your love, kindness and wisdom. I offer you, Infinite love and gratitude, my beloved teachers.

My journey into healing was guided by *Dr. Deepak Chopra, Dr. David Simon, Bri. Maya Tiwari and Debbie Ford* taking my yoga and meditation practices to the next level. In gratitude for their wisdom, workshops and books which helped me understand the connection between mind, body and spirit and the scientific application and validation of Ayurveda in modern times.

Enthralled by all this exposure, I learnt about Institute for Integrative Nutrition®. Meeting *Joshua Rosenthal* and enrolling in his program, was a *Déjà vu!* as well as a *Eureka!* moment for me. His teaching was simple yet profound; it resonated with me and reminded me of my days in Sugi's kitchen. I was able to learn from teachers like *Dr. Andrew Weil, Marc David, David Wolfe, Annemarie Colbin, Dr. Mark Hyman, Dr. Walter Willet* and *Dr. John Douillard* to name a few. Thank you *Joshua Rosenthal*, I was finally home with my tribe!

My *aadar* or sincere respect to my Hay House guides; *Louise Hays, Dr. Wayne Dyer, Doreen Virtue, Marianne Williamson, Dr. Brian Weis, Dr. Christian Northrup* and *Cheryl Richardson* whose work I have loved and admired for many years. In gratitude to the Balboa Press team, *Reid Tracy, Nancy Levin, Mollie Harrison, Nicole Osbun, Shawn Waggener, Andrew Carter* and *Maneli Reihani*. Thank you for creating this space in your publishing house for my little book.

I express my devotion or *anuraag* to my friends, my support system. *Dr. Shalini Saksena*, my friend, philosopher and guide, I thank you for your constant love, support and encouragement. *Mary Mahabir*, I thank you for accepting me in my financially torn and mutilated condition and having faith in me. *Fred Badalli, Nizara Juman* my dear friends for standing strong besides me when I needed you, *Sundri Mahtani* for your nurturing care during my first pregnancy, *Kala* and *Rashmi Hathiramani* for sharing their love of cooking, hospitality and home. I am in gratitude to *Piyush* and *Avanti Majmudar, Vinod* and *Puja Hiranandani,* for being a solid example of love and commitement in a marriage.

Thank you, *Michele Caws* for being my accountability partner as we both wrote our books. I cherish our working remotely, yet together at four o'clock in the morning. *Lindsey Smith*, thank you for joyfully leading the writing workshop. *Christi Molinari* thanks for sharing your knowledge of skincare ingredients and techniques.

Last but not the least, I offer my *Prema* or utmost love to my beloved husband *Sandeep*, children *Swati, Angad* and *Rangan*. Without your love, support, critique and compassion this book could not have been penned.

Above and beyond all, I bow down to the most important teacher in the Universe that dwells within us and is not separate from us. The journey from me to myself was a very long one. But when I met myself, I instantly recognized a long lost soul mate within, I said *I am Pratibha Masand Sachdev* and I am a radiant being of love and light. *Aham Bhramasmi! Kun Fayakun! I am that I am!* Thanks for living with me and within me. I greet you, I salute you, I embrace you, I acknowledge you; the beloved of my being.

Namaste! ...I love and honor you!

introduction....*parichay*

*I am a little pencil in the hand of a writing God,
who is sending a love letter to the world*
– Mother Teresa

In each one of us, dwells a still small voice, a source we call by different names. Some of us call it intuition, some call it guidance, and some call it the universe within. This simple book you hold in your hands offers messages of practical guidance I have received during this beautiful journey called life. It holds within its pages, suggestions for daily growth and sustenance. Some messages hold the recipes of cooking by spirit, nurturing through soul food, yet others of herbal recipes used for my skincare and also ingredients used for my personal exploration and spiritual growth.

I have personally experienced this guidance during my waking moments and my sleeping moments. This soft voice spoke to me when I was happily engaged in daily chores, when I cried in deepest anguish and as I lay on a sick bed too ill to stir. It led me each time to the pure core of my being, even in the murkiest moments of my life. A simple ordinary woman, I was led by this inner voice through extraordinary experiences. For this, I am eternally grateful to the Universe that resides within me.

This book is homage to my paternal grandmother *Sugi Boolchand Masand*. It was in her lap I learned the meaning of true radiance. I played with her in her kitchen, in the meadows, in the bazaars of Ulhasnagar; gathering herbs, cooking soul food, mixing simple ingredients for the nourishment of my mind, body and spirit. As I patiently persevered, I learned the true meaning of radiance that came from leading an organic life; loving and serving others without forgetting the self.

As I talk in depth about my culinary journey and my travels through various countries and continents, I share with you my moments of discovery, when each herb spoke to me and shared its own personal story. I also narrate my meeting and learning from various spiritual masters and my realization that our own radiance resides within us and is always ready to illuminate our path.

Too often we fail to see the sun that is lit within our soul, while we seek a lamp from others.

As I travelled on this journey of life, I learned that my life is a testimony of power of affirmative thinking and prayer. I gathered that I am here to play, to work, to love and to have faith; that in doing so Gods purpose for my life will keep unfolding itself. I understood that true work is accomplishment of something by hand, intellect and heart, which shall help others as much as it helps me. Play; the doing of something different from the routine, meditating, relaxing with a hobby, spending time in fresh air, in the woods, in my garden and in pleasant tasks like playing with my children always brought me great joy and kept me grounded and connected to earth.

I discovered that we all have a capacity to love. Love to me, in a broader sense is a desire to nurture, to share, to preserve, to protect; a feeling of deep affection. Faith means that I believe in God, a kind universe that loves me, and bears my troubles, as well as teaches me to bear them with grace. I now know that it is this faith which has given meaning to my work, grace to my spirit, sacrament to my love and direction to my life.

Now that you have chosen to read this book, I encourage you to embrace it by setting your intention. What is it you wish to find in these pages? Is it a cooking recipe, a skin care solution or just an elusive piece of life's puzzle? Understand that these are all interconnected. Your body mind and spirit all dance in unison as you follow the rhythm of life.

Note that this book is not intended to replace recommendations or advice from physicians or other healthcare providers. Rather it is intended to help you make informed decisions and choices about your health and well-being. Work hand in hand with your healthcare provider in a combined quest for optimal wellness. Not all the 108 recipes are showcased towards the end of the book; some are interwoven in the narrative of the various chapters. There are food recipes, skincare rituals and recipes and some word recipes to create empowering thoughts. They all come together to nurture our mind, body and spirit.

This book is not a treatise on Ayurveda. I am just a humble student of Ayurveda and other enriching holistic healthcare modalities, always eager to learn, share and be of service. This is hence a very humble offering of lessons I have learnt from my teachers, both external and the one residing within me; and applied in my life for self-nurture and self-healing.

I encourage you to joyfully experiment, to go within and explore the possibilities lying dormant within and as you step into the depth of your own inner universe, uncover the grace and good health that is your birthright. Your own recipe for good health and radiance awaits you; compound it, be your own pharmacist.

So dear one, explore and discover that healing light within you and *Let It Glow!*

prelude....*bhumika*

Eko Onkaar, Satnaam, Kartaar Purakh, Nirbhay Nirvair, Akaal Moorat, Ajooni Saihbhang, Gur Prasad, Jap Aad Sach, Jugaad Sach, Haibhi Sach, Nanik Hausi Bhi Sach!
— *Japji Sahib*

In the beginning, there was one universal creator, God. His name is truth. He is the infinite giver, a creative being personified, fearless and one without envy or hatred. Self-existing, He is gloriously formless. He is beyond birth and death and I meditate and chant on this infinite truth, which shall remain true forever and ever!
— *Japji Sahib*

With this Sikh prayer on her lips, my grandmother Sugi embarked on her journey to new horizons. This is her story of migration and settlement. The year was 1947, and the journey was from Shikarpur, Sindh in Pakistan to Ulhasnagar, Bombay in India. Many years later, these would be the same first words that she would utter in my ears when I was born. As did I, in the ears of my children, as they came into my arms in a foreign land, Bridgetown, Barbados.

Travelling to Bombay, India on the *Satpura*, a ship that brought refugees from Pakistan to newly independent India; Sugi came to India as a refugee along with her husband and eight surviving children. Having lived in the comfort and luxury of a large family estate, the new humble beginnings of re-establishing her life in a different city were very daunting as any refugee will testify. Armed with the ammunition of love and food, brought with her onboard the ship carrying the refugees, I later heard the stories about her offering food to other fellow travelers as she fed her own children. Various breads like *Mitho Lolo, Koki, Lolee, Besanreen, Dal and Mooriyah Payi Mani;* her soul foods had been packed in a tin and gilt container along with *Ambriyoon jyun Bidryun* or pickled raw mangoes, to add the sixth flavor and *Sundh ain Gidamari ji Chatreen* or a ginger and tamarind chutney for digestive comfort.

She knew from her cooking experience that these foods would last her for many days without spoiling on her long journey to Bombay. Cooked without any artificial preservatives and just with pure intentions, prayers and perseverance, these satisfied the hunger of her children and some other travelers. Before leaving Shikarpur, she went to bow down at the ancestral shrine of *Masand Gur Durbar,* offering and accepting the *Karah Prasad* a sacred whole wheat offering. Many years later, this was one of the first recipes she shared with me, guiding me gently as I made this very special *Prasad* or a sacred offering.

As I grew older many delicious recipes were shared with me. I learnt more by watching her and my aunts, asking questions and following their simple directions. During the Sindhi festivals of *Thadri* or *Satai*, these foods were made a day ahead and *Sigri* or the earthen stove was not lit on the day of prayers. This was so that the women could have a day of rest from cooking and lighting a stove.

Widowed within a couple of years of moving to Bombay, Sugi was faced with taking care of a large family. Undaunted by the task that lay ahead of her, she met life head-on; finding joy in daily household chores of gathering and grinding the herbs and grains, cooking for and nourishing her family. Very resourceful, she knew how to extract the best from each herb, ingredient and use it in multiple ways.

She had taught her daughters to read, write, sew and knit early on. They in turn became experts at sewing and ran a *Shaala* or sewing school for young girls in the area. Teaching *Sindhi* and *Gurumukhi* script to other displaced refugee children who might have otherwise lost the touch with their mother tongue; her daughters forged a life for themselves independent of any external support. Helping their mother raise their four younger brothers and a sister, they chose a life of devotion and simplicity, each one eventually rising in their chosen field of work. There was a strong theme of independent women in my life who triumphed using what life gave them; and this was to be my legacy.

Where did my grandmother's strength come from? What was her secret? Regardless of how good or bad she perceived experiences of her life to be, she had realized that they would have never happened in the first place if not meant for her highest good. She accepted what happened as the perfect synchronicity of her life. She believed that life had always been perfect and always will be. Therein lay her source of strength; in her faith, surrender and acceptance of the divine will in her life. Somewhere along the line, she was chiseling these thoughts in the soft rock of my mind and creating a sculpture that would withstand the onslaught of the emotional earthquake of wind, water and fire to come.

These recipes that I share with you are interspersed throughout the narrative and they culminate towards the end of this book, as we conclude this journey together. Homemade, simple and intuitively made with love and reverence, these food recipes may not be low in calories; but just a little is required to satiate our mind, body and spirit.

*Do not surrender your grief so quickly, let it cut
more deeply, let it ferment and season you as few human
or divine ingredients can. Something is missing from
my heart tonight that has made my eyes so soft and my
voice so tender and my need of God so absolutely clear
– Hafiz.*

background....*prashthabhumi*

The world we knew as children is still buried within our minds. Our childlike self is the deepest level of our being. It is who we really are, and what is real doesn't go away
– Marianne Williamson

I was born in Ulhasnagar, Bombay, India in a simple Sindhi family and raised by a very liberated, forward thinking paternal grandmother Sugi, and my paternal aunts, her daughters and her daughters-in-law. I had arrived early to two very young parents. A mother, just nineteen, was not ready for a baby and a father, just a few years older than her was unsure of how to balance it all.

I arrived five weeks prematurely, in quite a rush. I was Sugi's first grandchild, and she stood beside my mother ready to welcome me as the German lady doctor was summoned. She narrated many years later, that a slippery tiny little bundle, I oozed out of my mother's womb, all slimy and bloody; into the doctors hands and landed straight into her heart. She affirmed that I did not cry; I just opened my blue grey eyes, looked around and gurgled. This confirmed what I remembered of my birthing process, of opening my eyes and seeing an extension of a pink, warm, comforting glow.

I was very little when my mom handed me over to my grandmother Sugi, and headed for her parents' home citing differences with my father. Once my grandma's arms embraced me there was no returning. I guess I looked at my grandma and knew that I was safe and sound and this was where I had chosen to come for a very specific reason. While there, I had various teachers to meet and many lessons to learn.

I slept adjacent to our prayer room which housed our *Guru Granth Sahibji*. Every morning I awoke to the chanting of prayers by my eldest aunt Devi and the aroma of Sugi cooking her morning meals.

The gentle aroma of incense and camphor being lit and *Karah Prasad*, sweet whole wheat offering being made on *Chand Raat* or new noon, is one of my fondest memories. After the prayers, I was always eager to go distribute the *Prasad* to my neighbors; and they waited eagerly every month for this. It did not matter what their religion or caste was, I went with this loving offering and they accepted it with love and joy. This was always followed by the *Bairanoh Sahib* or ritual of offering the grains and immersion of the same at the *Ulhās* river. Singing of *Jhulelal* bhajans as the friendly procession proceeded to the river was a beautiful sight to behold.

The new moon signified new beginning and hence the gratitude procession and celebration. *Jhulelal* a deity worshiped by the Sindhi's all over the world is a deity of oceans and Sindhi's being a community of traders and travelers worshiped him for safe sea travels. As I share various recipes later, I will narrate the role of different ingredients, chants and prayers as they applied in creating a life of radiance.

Sugi's mornings began at four o'clock in her kitchen, preparing food for her family. She chanted and prayed as she cooked. This she said raised the vibration of the food. As everyone awoke and left for work, she handed them their lunch tins and snacks. *Tiffin's* also went to children in the neighborhood whose parents were unwell.

Until I started my formal school education, I tagged behind her as she shopped for fresh vegetables and gathered herbs and fresh spices. I would watch her closely as she gathered, tore, crushed, ground and tasted each herb and spice; explaining to me their medicinal properties, aroma and flavor quotient in cooking and herbal preparations for skin and body care.

Watching her as she cleaned and washed grains before drying and grinding, I asked her countless questions. The first lesson she taught me was to pray before I even started the preparation to cook. We prayed over grains, pulses, vegetables, coal and even the *Sigri* or the stove we cooked on. She would ask me to lovingly run my hands through various grains, feel the plumpness of juicy fruits, and experience the tartness of pickles.

I learnt to handle all my cooking utensils with love and respect, to treat fuel or fire with awe and care, to treat food with grace and as a blessing. Cooking therefore holds a very sacred place in my life and my relationship with the food is that of reverence. Cooking to me is an expression of my love for all who consume the meal I cook.

Even after I started my formal schooling, I remember running home in the afternoon after school and helping her gather the *papad or* dehydrated lentil crackers, *kachri* or dehydrated wafers and *achaar* or pickles that lay drying out in the sun. The evening meal was prepared on an old fashioned coal burning s*igri,* slow cooked to perfection. As she chanted and praised, expressing the gratitude for the meal, I watched her radiant face glowing like the ambers she stoked to keep the fire lit. I wondered as a child, the recipe for her radiance. Now I know it!

The women in the family would gather around and share the chores, sometimes happily and other times not so happily. I was taken under the wings of various aunts who had several different skill sets. Each came with a different flair and flavor, each more radiant in her own light; offering me, a tasty morsel of nourishment from their delectable dish of life.

From my prayerful aunt Devi, I learned to recite, chant mantras and prayers which she herself did effortlessly. She could recite *Bhagwad Geeta*, a Hindu scripture and *Sundar Gutko* a Sikh spiritual text by heart. I know that she was instrumental in my choosing my thesis topic as I completed my Master's degree in History from Bombay University. The research done for my dissertation on literary significance of Hindu scripture *Ramcharitmanas* helped me later in life when I was able to surmount many difficulties with a chant on my lips and smile on my face. As I learnt various spiritual practices, I was being strengthened and prepared, I was to realize this much later.

From my dearest aunt Radha I learnt to love freely and unconditionally; I am proud to be known in our close circles as *Radha ji baby* or Radha's child. She taught me to stand tall in a world where women were just coming of age. Her love taught me to trust and serve without reservations. This stood to benefit me later when I had to build new lasting relationships in Barbados, a country foreign to me. I reached a new country, where I knew no one, yet when I left it twelve years later, I had built friendships that have supported me and lasted me a lifetime.

From my fiercely independent aunt Shanta, I learnt to be self-sufficient and later how to stand up for myself. She was a witness to my life in Barbados and encouraged me to speak my mind and stand up for myself. She reminded me to look for alternate solutions and polish my inborn talents and pursue my dreams. This is exactly what I did when I started painting t-shirts and writing articles in magazines, to put food on the table. I learnt to find the work I loved as well to love the work I found.

From my youngest aunt Pushpa, I learnt discipline and importance of hygiene and physical activity. She is a stickler for cleanliness; today my home reflects her lessons of organization and discipline.

From my nurturing aunt Chandra, I imbibed her passion for ethnic cooking. She cooked with a passion and her dining table was always a display of an eye appealing, lip smacking and tongue tickling spread. I learnt from her the skills of food presentation.

I learnt from my beautiful aunt Maina, her efficacious and timeless skin care beauty recipes, as well as continental cooking. She is an epitome of classic beauty and grace. She shared that although grace and beauty is inherently present in each one of us, we still need to polish it. I learnt the first lessons of self-care, from her.

Durga, my simplest aunt on the other hand, taught me how to accomplish more with less. These women together, polished the various facets of my being, preparing me for what lay ahead of me.

Apart from cooking, I was introduced to many other health promoting natural therapies very early in my life. For example, every night before Sugi went to bed, she washed her face, hands and feet, paying special attention to her feet. She would sponge her feet with a wet linen wash cloth and massage them with coconut, sesame or mustard oil, depending on the season. This she said allowed the feet to receive the intuitive correspondence from mother earth for the well-being of whole body. She gently explained to me that wellness and the ability to heal are dependent upon the unimpeded movement of energy. As I later learned in my Ayurvedic training, the circulation of *prana* is facilitated via the *chakras* or a network of fine energy pathways called *nadis*.

Her cleansers and moisturizers were simple, made from ingredients right in her kitchen. I share some of the skin care recipes I have collected over a period of time, throughout the book and particularly towards the end along with some food recipes. As she nourished her family with her cooking, she set a good example of self-care and self-nurture.

Saturday nights, she would soak and gently boil *Arishtha's* or soap nuts in a large pot. This soapy liquid was used the next day for gently shampooing of our hair. *Neem* twigs were picked in the evening and soaked overnight in a large glass of water; upon waking up next morning we would chew on a stick, turning it into a fibrous brush. This I learnt was the world's first natural tooth brush, tooth paste and mouthwash combined in one. The wonderful anti-bacterial, anti-viral and antiseptic qualities of *Neem* are now well researched and documented.

Every summer I was encouraged to visit relatives and friends in different parts of the country, sometimes traveling with her and at other times with my aunts. Learning spirituality from a pilgrimage, history and geography from traveling first hand, she said was better than just reading about it in books. This brings back memories of two such memorable vacations.

It was during a summer vacation about forty years ago, that I visited the small sleepy little village of Shirdi as a young girl. A pilgrimage to many visitors; this was the land Shirdi Sai Baba had called his home. It was about four o'clock in the morning as I sleepily followed my aunt and her friends to visit the temple for *Aarti* or morning prayers. A cold water shower had still not woken me up. As our aunts walked ahead, a friend and I found ourselves lost. Terrified, we did not see a soul in sight as we stopped to find our way. As we looked around in pitch dark of the early morning, we were approached by an older gentleman; as he came closer he just smiled, he had the kindest eyes I could ever remember seeing. He gestured and pointed us towards a direction, as he was chanting a mantra or a prayer. Bedazzled by his radiance we thanked him for his kindness and had just walked a few steps, as we saw that our aunts had rushed back to see where we had stopped. As they approached us, we told them about the gentleman who had guided us a minute ago. We all turned to look at the direction he had just walked away, but there was no one in sight. It was a miraculous intervention we all agreed.

Another vacation that stood out in my mind was when I attended a wedding. I remember as a young girl visiting our distant relatives and family friends in a small town in Central India. Upon waking each morning I would find a handful of jasmine flowers on my pillow, in fact I woke up to the aroma of jasmine flowers. No one was able to tell me how these flowers got to my pillow every morning without fail and I didn't learn the truth until many years later.

I learnt a lot at my conventional convent school and University, but the lessons learnt in my home, from my elders were the most valuable lessons that no degree conferred on me could teach me. I learnt to pray before I cook and express gratitude for the bountiful spread when I sit down to eat. This put me in an ideal state of digestion, assimilation and later elimination. I was reminded that there is a physical body and then there is an energetic body, and keeping them in balance was of utmost importance. I was reminded at each step to make 'love' the main ingredient in each recipe, whether it was in food, skincare or my thoughts. Most importantly I was taught to nurture and nourish the community I lived in, my family and above all myself. My conventional education gave me the tools to make a living, but the loving education imparted to me at home has given me my life.

Sugi's home had become my home and refuge; until the day of my departure to London after my arranged marriage, on board the British Airways flight twenty one years later. A few months before that fateful day, I had bid her farewell as she went on to the other realm becoming my guardian angel forever and always. The lessons I learnt from her, guide my existence even to this day. As I pour the perfume of her essence onto others today, I experience a lingering aroma of her fragrance on my fingers and in my soul.

> *I am adventurous; I walk through the doorways of courage and enter a new world of wonder and awe. I discover that I have nothing to fear, for my explorations lead me to treasure chests that have always existed inside of me*
> *– Doreen Virtue*

introspection....*atmaparikshan*

Whatever relationships you have attracted in your life at this moment, are precisely the ones you need in your life at this moment. There is a hidden meaning behind all events, and this hidden meaning is serving your own evolution
– Dr. Deepak Chopra

It was an unusually cold night in November aboard a British Airways flight to Heathrow, London. Warm serviettes and snacks didn't help assuage the cold damp feeling of apprehension that had suddenly set in. A new chapter of my life was unfolding; twenty one, I was embarking on a journey to a new horizon, unexplored vistas and views. I was on my way to the Caribbean, via London. Newly married and still uncertain about how the pages would turn in this new chapter of my life, I sighed as I saw the bright lights of Bombay recede beneath the clouds. Something just didn't feel right and I shrugged it off as an apprehension of a newlywed mind. My first time flying ever, that too on an International flight to an International destination, first time away from my close knit overprotective family.

As the bone chilling winds greeted me in London, I was warmed by the hospitality of our hosts. The ambiance and comfort of an elegant hotel in Marble Arch was great, and my day was spent with relatives and friends eager to meet the by now not so newlyweds. As the novelty of visiting relatives and friends in London and Edinburgh wore off; I was tired and ready to go home. Seeing that home was now many thousand miles behind, I realized that I had to move forward. In all the hectic post wedding rituals and travel activities, I realized I had missed my period. Cold, chilled to the bone, tired I wept as I had no one to share this news with and seek counsel.

I arrived in beautiful Barbados at the newly renovated Sir Grantley Adams International Airport. Greeted by Steel Pan music, the sweet salty air was a warm welcome after freezing London temperatures. This was the place I would call home for next twelve years, learning some of the toughest lessons of my life. The aroma of Frangipani flowers filled the air as we drove past the beautiful beaches. Although it was already dark, I could hear the sound of waves crashing on the shores and I saw a soft glimpse of the ocean.

Awakening the next morning, I realized that I was on my own, in a foreign country, with no friends and family. From the noise and sounds of busy Bombay life, I was thrown into a house with deafening silence as my now ex-husband become preoccupied with work. He travelled intensely, sometimes for many weeks on end. Alone, pregnant, and away from all the comforts of familiar sights and faces, I would try calling home in Mumbai. This was in the early eighties and trunk calls took three to five days to connect. I had a rationed time of three minutes per call, every three months; no more.

Before leaving India, I had suggested carrying at least some spices and cooking utensils but was told that they were readily available in London and we would buy them from Southhall. This did not happen and upon reaching Barbados, I saw an empty pantry and unfamiliar cooking utensils. Newly pregnant I craved my favorite foods. Nourishment of every kind was evading me as I continued to nourish a little life in my womb. As I met other Indians living on the Island, I learnt that they all shopped for their spices either while on their trip to India or when they went for vacation or business to England or America. Spices and herbs were not available on the Islands, I was told by my Indian friends. I was truly surprised as I had learnt in school about the abundance of spices in the Caribbean.

One weekend, on an invitation of some friends, we went for a picnic to Welchman Hall Gully, a natural trail in the parish of St. Thomas. As everyone walked chatting about day to day business of living, I walked slowly looking at the ground; there was a distinct aroma in the air that I recognized. Suddenly out of the corner of my eye, I caught sight of a strange mud covered nut. I picked it up and cleaned it gently to reveal a nutmeg. Astonished, I looked around, bending to pick various spices strewn on the ground. Quickly I gathered all the cardamoms, nutmegs and cloves that I found on the ground and collected them in my scarf, tying up a neat little bundle.

My joy knew no bounds as I hugged the trees; I asked my friends if they knew what I had collected. They peeked into my scarf, looked at my mud covered collection and asked me why I was playing with dirt. I came home and washed the spices, cleaned them thoroughly and the next day dried them in the sun. I joyfully chanted and sang as I roasted them in the oven along with some store bought spices like whole black peppercorns, cinnamon bark and bay leaves. As I ground it in a small electric grinder, the aroma of my first home made *garam masalo* or Indian allspice floated in the air of my kitchen.

I craved familiar herbs, condiments and their aromas and my favorite *sao masalo* green garlic, cilantro and mint sauce was becoming a distant reality. Cilantro was one such ingredient I really missed, but those days it was not readily available. As I travelled to various Islands like Guyana, Suriname, Trinidad and Tobago, I saw vast vegetation and a flourishing Indian population. These were the descendants of the first Indian settlers who had arrived in on the ship *Komagata Maru* many years ago. Away from home, they had created their own little India, creating their own recipes reminiscent of their heritage. I finally found the famous delectable and delicious Indo-Caribbean cuisine like *Caribbean Curry Powder, Roti, Dahlpuri, Doubles, Choka and Philourie.*

One day as a relative asked me to make a traditional meal, while I visited them in Trinidad; I asked his wife for cilantro along with some other herbs and spices needed to create it. She responded that cilantro was not available on the island. On the previous evening as I had stepped into her wild overgrown backyard, I had seen a large leafy overgrowth which looked very familiar. On asking her help, a young Trinidadian girl of Indian descent, I was told that it was *bandaniya,* a popular aromatic herb, used for flavoring by the locals. I went into her backyard again and I took a wild leaf and crushed it between my fingers; it released a heartwarming aroma of cilantro. The leaf was a little larger and aroma a little stronger, but I joyfully realized that I had found an abundance of *ban dhaniya* or wild cilantro.

By this time I had started experimenting with various locally grown herbs and spices. I started recreating those familiar aromas and tastes in my kitchen and reveling in this new found joy of cooking with different hitherto unfamiliar ingredients. As each herb spoke to me and narrated its story, I listened raptly and gathered its essence. Just like Sugi, I did not measure, I just tasted, and intuitively cooked with love, chanting and praying while I cooked. Sometimes, these dishes tasted fine and at other times, plates flew in my direction and I was pronounced to be a good for nothing, useless cook. My kitchen had become my refuge and I continued my experimentation and exploration.

All the promises made prior to the wedding, kept crashing. My dream of pursuing a PhD was crushed as we were informed about the high cost of college fees. I also learnt that behind the façade of joy and laughter of the happy go lucky couples, lay many bruised hearts. Pining for love in their marriage, many young women accepted the presence of other women in their lives or chose to be that other woman since they could not find solace and love in their own marriages. All this was very foreign and unacceptable to my sheltered psyche. No one had prepared me for this painful acceptance of a divided life. I could see all around me that, the physical bruises were easy to hide and quick to heal, it was much more difficult to heal from the emotional wounds.

I was surprised at the generosity of many kind folks. As soon as they learnt about my pregnancy they offered me their precious spices laced with their wisdom of leading a successful life on a small Island. As I prepared for my delivery, I was not prepared for the arrival of a premature baby. Swati arrived five weeks early, just like I had. Her birth brought an immense joy to my life; I now had a companion who I loved and knew would love me. My whole life revolved around her as she taught me things that only a child can teach a parent. My unhappy existence had a meaning now. For first time in Barbados, I was really happy.

My overjoyed father commented on the phone after her birth, that I now had the opportunity to do my PhD in human development. He left us soon after that for his heavenly abode. A trunk call summoned me home as he suffered a severe heart attack. Taking my little baby, I travelled back to India to see him and grant him the joy of seeing his first grandchild. He passed away peacefully in his bed at home, after we brought him home from Jaslok hospital. Not wanting to burden my aunts with dismal news of my ailing marriage, I returned to Barbados after a month.

Hoping that things would improve, I decided to give my marriage my all. Reminding myself that after all it was a marriage of two families and I did not want to disappoint anyone. I put aside my own pain and anguish as I immersed myself in teaching little children the art of singing and dancing. As I helped organize *Diwali* shows and other events, I realized that I could either wallow in self-pity or joyously share my talents with others; I chose to do the latter. I watched many young children blossom into happy dancers; which brought immense pleasure to my otherwise lackluster life. Many years later a friend shared that one of those shy little children had blossomed into a talented dancer and received an award for recreating a piece

I had taught him as a child. I was told that he reminisced about his childhood and acknowledged my guidance as he was presented with his award on stage. My heart was filled with joy and pride to know of his success. When touched with love and care, even the hardest kernels yield flourishing crops.

As I welcomed the birth of our son Angad, my ex-husband decided to start his own business and asked me to join the staff and work at the new store. With no previous experience of running a business, I was not at all prepared for this turn of events. I was literally thrown into business, further crushing my dreams of an academic career. As I tried to balance home and work, I realized to everyone's surprise including my own that I was a natural at it. As I gained more confidence in running the business, I could not close my eyes to financial mistakes being made. Clearly, we did not see eye to eye on anything and could not carry on together any further. This painful realization created further divide and anguish.

As I tried to deal with this anguish, I did not want to hit the bottle as I had seen some other unhappy women resort to, nor did I want to give up on my life as few others had done in their moment of desperation. At this weakest moment of my life, I turned to praying and meditating earnestly, finding solace in spirituality. I would attend miracle services in a church nearby, seeking a miraculous intervention. Transcendental meditation and yoga entered at this time in my life, unveiling the strength that had been hidden within me all along.

To sort my thoughts, I decided to take my children and visit India for a much needed break after many years. While in India, I visited Shirdi and then Puttaparthi. I remember that the temperature in Puttaparthi that day was a hundred degrees and we were already late for the morning *Darshan*. We decided to wait for the afternoon *Darshan*; while I waited I decided to donate a small amount at the trust office. After writing a check I left the trust office to wait in the shade of a large tree.

I knew we had to return for Bangalore that evening itself and was eager to have a glimpse of Sri Satya Sai Baba. As everyone rushed in for the afternoon *Darshan* before four o'clock, I found myself struggling to get inside with a child in my arms and another in tow. I decided to wait outside, finding myself almost last to enter the grounds. As I entered, an elderly lady who was distributing tokens for row seating, asked me to pick a token from the closed bag. As I pulled a token I was astounded to see number one. Tears running down my face, I sat right in front of the door my Baba came through. As he came near, he lovingly came closer and blessed us. Upon my return home, I received a note from the trust in Puttaparthi. Enclosed along with note was the check I had written as a donation. It had been returned to me along with a note that said, your need at this time is greater. My Baba knew my financial condition better than any close relative or friend.

Broke and saddened, one night as I sat rocking myself on a rocking chair in my children's bedroom after a huge bitter exchange, I prayed for an answer. As I sat praying that night, I experienced a large pink cloud of glowing warm radiance enter the room. I felt the comforting and loving arms of a very loving universe hug me. I heard a whisper, do what you are guided to do, be as compassionate and loving as I am with you. As I fell asleep in the comforting arms of my father God, I promised myself to follow through with this guidance.

I calmly and compassionately requested my ex-husband for a divorce explaining that we were unequally yoked and did not deserve to be unhappy together. I also realized that I did not have money, so I looked at the possibility of finding alternate means of income. I started a small wearable art business, painting t-shirts all night for a friend, who distributed them to the larger department stores. I remember Swati and Angad sitting and studying while I painted, at night. Swati's little hands helping me at times with various chores and Angad regaling us with his antics and jokes. We experienced grace in the form of laughter and joy that we tried to bring into our otherwise mundane existence.

I also started selling some of my jewelry along with furniture and appliances of the house in preparation of paying off the remaining debt and buying tickets for our return to India. I picked up my pen and started writing and contributing articles to a local magazine. As I prepared to leave with my children, I often thought of my mother and her anguish in her married life. I was able to understand her wanting out of an unhappy marriage, but I could not still fathom her decision to leave me behind.

I struggled with the thought of the stigma my children would have to face, once we moved to India. What must have gone through my mother's mind who was just nineteen when she gave me up? For the first time since her departure, I missed her presence in my life. I was standing on the same threshold that she had once crossed, to start a new life. In retrospect, today I thank her for the blessing of her absence, for it allowed me to learn many valuable lessons.

As soon as I had enough saved for the travel tickets, I decided to leave for India along with my children. He, I suppose, believing that we would be back after a short vacation, decided to join us. I felt a deep compassion for him and I could see that we both were victims of a social system that was in the throes of a huge upheaval.

As I ventured forward, I realized that I had learned a beautiful lesson of living in faith and forgiving with compassion. I have chosen to exclude from my narrative, many experiences which were the source of extreme pain during this time in my life. This is because I have come to a place of complete peace and understanding of the situations that unfolded and the lessons which were necessary. Although this does not diminish the anguish that I experienced, my journey of self-discovery has allowed me to view things in a kinder, more compassionate light. I have understood that forgiveness of those who hurt us and self-forgiveness of mistakes made are necessary for the balance required for inner radiance.

> *With everything that has happened to you, you can either feel sorry for yourself, or treat what has happened as a gift. Everything is either an opportunity to grow, or an obstacle to keep you from growing. You get to choose*
> *– Dr. Wayne Dyer*

regrowth....*punarviddhi*

*You do not meet your loved ones by accident or coincidence.
Destiny delicately dictates the rediscovery of your immortal love*
— *Dr. Brian Weiss*

En route to India, I had decided to spend a few days with my cousin in New York. It was here that destiny was to change the course of my life. While we spent a couple of days in New York, Sandeep a family friend who had learnt about my trip back to India, expressed his desire to come and visit me. I had last seen him about thirteen years ago and was happy to meet him when he drove down from Pennsylvania. While he visited with us, an untimely snowstorm brewed on the horizon. My cousin asked him to stay over as the roads to Pennsylvania were getting very icy. He decided to accept their invitation and as we chatted late in the night reminiscing about our childhood, I shared that I was on my way to finalize my divorce and start afresh in India. Saddened about my situation, he offered to help me if needed. I brushed aside his request and thanked him for his kindness.

Things had changed in Bombay; it now had a new name, Mumbai. Or should I say that it had reverted to its old name, shrugging off the name given by the British. To my utmost disappointment, my family refused to support me in my decision to divorce. They felt it was a marriage of two families and would bring stigma to the family. My parents' divorce many years ago was brought up constantly and thrown in my face. After much persuasion and many tearful discussions, my divorce was finalized a day before Valentine's Day and I was granted the custody of my children.

Later that year, Sandeep visited India for his annual trip. He invited us to his family home in Central India. I joyfully agreed to travel with the children for a well-deserved vacation. While he showered the kids with love and affection, playing games with them and reading stories to them; I enjoyed cooking with his grandmother Indira and relearning some old dishes with a little modern twist. An exceptional cook, her culinary talent was well-known and respected in the family. My first *Satpuro* was made under her directions many years earlier on one of her visits to Ulhasnagar. While she rejoiced in sharing her history, I realized that the common thread of the partition of 1947 had seamlessly transformed many friendships to the extent that one did not know where the friendship ended and the relationship began.

I knew that a young divorcee with children is not a welcome sight at family functions in small towns, but I was not prepared for the onslaught of deep digs and uncouth queries. While I was lovingly greeted by Sandeep's grandparents and aunts, I was astounded to see others in the circle regard us with suspicion. As unsavory comments were dropped about our friendship, I realized that I did not want his short visit with his family to be marred with unpleasantness. As I readied to leave with the children, he asked me to stay. Upon his insistence that night, we decided to go for a walk after dinner. As we walked and chatted, he picked a few jasmine flowers from a neighboring shrub and placed them in my hands. As the memory of many years ago resurfaced, he confessed that the jasmine I found on my pillow on waking up many years ago had been placed by him every morning before I woke up. He said that he was young and in his teens at that time and did not know how to express his love for someone clearly older than him. In utter disbelief, I remember bursting into laughter as I asked him if he was crazy.

As he joined us on our trip back to Mumbai, I was further perplexed when he asked me to marry him. I was a little shaken and told him that I had never perceived him in that light and that I was in too much pain already to give it a serious thought. Upon reaching Mumbai, I realized that gossip about his affection for us had preceded us. Saddened by the turn of events I discussed this with a close friend, confidante and guide. While supporting me completely, she encouraged me to dig deep within and seek my answers.

I prayed for an answer, and I was guided to take a bold and previously unthought-of step. After discussing and weighing this situation with my children, I decided that we would move and give ourselves a chance to reconstruct our happiness.

When we arrived in Pennsylvania, we were greeted by an exuberant and happy young man. His joy radiated from his being as he embraced us all. He once again proposed marriage. I knew then that all this was predestined and was meant to be; I had to take action and respond to the joyous invitation of a new life. We saw that our love story was being woven like a jasmine garland that needed many knots to hold the delicate flowers till it was ready for the deity within our beings. Once our mind was made up, I remember sharing our decision with Swati and Angad. Overjoyed, Angad happily put his arms around Sandeep and said now I can call him Daddy! We were married shortly after that.

Once again I was on alien soil, learning to acclimatize to new weather and food changes. Food here was available in abundance and the portions were large, pizzas, pastas and other heavy foods became a norm. Although readily available in big states like New York and New Jersey, Indian groceries were not available in the Hershey or Harrisburg area those days. I remember fondly our monthly trips to Edison, New Jersey and Jackson Heights, New York. That was the only way we could bring Indian groceries home. Both Sandeep and I loved to cook, so we would cook up a storm in our kitchen, inviting our friends over. As the children watched us cook and experiment with different ingredients, they picked up cooking effortlessly.

While in Bombay, I had pursued a course in cosmetology so I could work from home while I waited for a suitable job at a local college. Since I already had that certification, I decided to continue that course in Pennsylvania and joined a cosmetology school. I discovered a new found passion for skin care and became a licensed aesthetician. This was followed by learning and teaching electrolysis in my cosmetology school. A whole new world of Advanced Skincare, Nutrition, Ayurveda, Yoga, Meditation, Reiki, Reflexology, Massage Therapy, Emotional Freedom Technique and Affirmations, opened up for me.

This led to my opening a day spa and wellness center and eventually my skincare education culminated into my receiving the prestigious CIDESCO diploma, world's most prestigious qualification in the field of Aesthetics and Beauty Therapy. I worked long hours at the wellness center nurturing my clients. As I helped others navigate their journey into wellness, one thing led to another and soon I found myself physically very tired but excited to be traveling on this road to further self-exploration and service.

A health crisis at this time brought me face to face with some hard choices. Did I want the recommended surgery for my multiple spinal herniation's issues or would I choose a road less travelled of healing myself naturally with various alternative modalities available? As I lay on my bed immobilized with severe pain, I was informed that I could lose the movements of my limbs. I chose the latter and on this journey to healing I was blessed with many teachers who held my hand and introduced me to the healing power within me. I learnt that my body had innate wisdom and if I listened to its guidance; I would be whole and healed.

As I healed my body through various alternate modalities, I dove deeper into the ocean of knowledge and self-discovery and I found many pearls of wisdom. Sometimes I had to gently open a soft shell to reveal a pearl and while at other times I had to struggle and pry open the securely hidden pearls. The more I learnt, the simpler the recipes and the route became. I reconnected with Ayurveda at this time. Drawn from Ayurvedic principles, my cooking recipes became simpler; I cooked more and more from spirit. I went back to nourishing Sindhi soul food of my childhood and found joy in reconnecting with my ancestors through these recipes.

I rediscovered that while a healthy organic diet was extremely important, my emotions as I prepared and consumed that food were equally significant.

I explored the world of organic living; simplified my skin care regime and went back to the earthiness of natural and organic food and skincare. I travelled within to find the answers for the previously evading radiance. My spiritual practices became simpler and simpler, giving way to further self-exploration and ultimately self-acknowledgment. I realized that while prayer helped me immensely to seek God's guidance, meditation brought me all the answers that I needed. While on this journey, I overhauled my lifestyle and stripped myself naked, allowing myself to be vulnerable. Most of the times it was painful, but the end results were miraculous.

Since I did not have the energy to cook big meals, my cooking became simplified. We cooked simple one pot meals that were easy to cook and even my children started cooking these simple meals on the weekends.

During this healing process, on one pitch dark and cold winter night in Pennsylvania, I woke up to a soft, gentle sound. After being bed ridden for many days, I surprised myself as I rose and walked slowly to my bedroom window. I moved the curtains off the window, or was it a veil over my eyes that I removed. A radiant, glowing pink sky greeted me; I turned and looked with wonder back into my room. Everything was glowing pink; a gentle radiance permeated everything. My body, felt weightless and transparent. I felt a sheer sense of joy, peace and serenity as I looked at my husband Sandeep, fast asleep on our bed. I remember walking into my children's room, wherever I went, the radiant glow completely surrounded me and walked with me. There was no pain or stiffness and I was feeling intense joy. As I raised my hands to say a prayer of gratitude, I realized I could see right through my pink glowing hands and I heard a soft whisper, have compassion for yourself as you share your gifts. Love yourself as you love others.

As my body, mind and spirit vibrated with this cosmic orgasm, I was in pure bliss. I realized that compassion and love for self are the most important ingredients in the recipe of life. To lead a radiant life, we need to nurture and love ourselves first. For too long I had numbed myself with food and other diversions, covering my deep pain of rejection by first my mother, then my ex-husband and later my present in-laws. But at this moment all was resolved, I felt a deep sense of love for everyone and above all for myself. I was immersed completely in immense joy, love and peace. In the unspoken words, I heard a truth in the message that the universe had for me as I accepted myself and experienced my own healing. *Love thyself!*

This is not just my journey, it is a journey of every living being that is evolving and growing in faith. A lesson in trusting, that in surrendering to the divine will is hidden the secret to our grace and radiance. This is a simple narrative of a journey of an ordinary woman who was privileged to have extraordinary experiences. It is my journey of transforming my life from a period to an exclamation!

> *You surrender to a lot of things which are not worthy of you. I wish you would surrender to your radiance, your integrity, your beautiful human grace.*
> *-Yogi Bhajan*

nurture....*posharn*

The more I observed human behavior, the more convinced I became that the key to health is understanding each person's individual needs, rather than following a set of predetermined rules. I saw plenty of evidence that having happy relationships, fulfilling career, an exercise routine and a spiritual practice are even more important than a daily diet
– Joshua Rosenthal

As I heard Joshua Rosenthal talk in Manhattan, New York, my mind travelled to a distant land, my home town of Ulhasnagar, Mumbai. I had heard these same thoughts expressed by my elders many years ago. All the memories flooded through my mind as I recalled various lessons learnt in my childhood. As we explored over one hundred dietary theories, I looked at the possibility of combining all this knowledge with my aesthetic education. I understood that there are many components in the recipe of achieving good health. Well-nourished skin is possible only if you have a well-nourished gut and a well-nourished spirit.

I had explored the teachings in the west and was grateful for learning a scientific approach to healing. It was time now to turn and seek once again from my roots and relearn the long forgotten lessons of ancient wisdom. I was drawn towards Ayurveda and its whole body, mind and spirit approach to healing the whole being. As I took a break to restore my health, I started to reconnect with some teachers from past and found some teachers like Melanie Sachs, right here in my own home. The complexity of Sanskrit words had already been effortlessly solved in my childhood, when Dada Kishinchand explained in Sindhi or Hindi the simple application of Ayurveda in our day to day living. For me Ayurveda was not a complicated science but the very art of living in balance. I encouraged my family to join me on this journey into wellness.

As I started romancing the herbs; each herb I fell in love with, led me to its potent secret core. Turmeric or *Haldi* told me many stories of calming the inflammations both in the gut and on the skin. Ginger or *Adrak* goaded me to ignite the digestive fire. Cloves or *Lavang* and cinnamon or *Dalchini* were revitalizing me with their spicy aromas while building the immunity of my skin. Cilantro or *Dhaniya* was calming my internal organs while supporting the regulation of my circulatory system. Azadirachta indica or *Neem* was purifying my skin, improving its resilience while it also added freshness to my breath. Basil or *Tulsi*, a holy plant found in every household in India was oxygenating my blood while purifying my skin. Spices like nutmegs, cardamoms, bay leaves, cumin danced in my saucepans as jasmine, roses and marigolds sang their sweet secret melodies in my skincare recipes. I was having the party of my life time as I nurtured and healed myself.

As I joyfully connected with my spirit, my kitchen became my temple. I sang, I chanted, I chopped, I kneaded, and I basically woke up to my limitless potential for healing my own body. My senses were delighting in the pleasure my body was receiving through these herbs, flowers and spices. I was reconnecting with my ancestors through these old recipes. The joyful moments spent in my grandma's kitchen were being recreated in my own kitchen with my children and husband. I was ready to cook a grand feast for the Universe.

My prayers were answered as my beloved teacher; Amma Srimad Sai Rajarajeshwari Devi visited America. I was assigned the honor of cooking meals for her. As she lovingly accepted my offering, overwhelmed with joy, I wept remembering the story of Lord Rama and Shabari, from epic *Ramayana* and *Ramcharitmanas*. A simple villager, Shabari was overjoyed when her beloved Lord Rama visited her in the forest during his exile. She collected wild berries in her scarf and ran to feed him. Not knowing if the berries were sweet or sour, she bit into each before offering Rama only the sweet ones. Lord Rama acknowledged her love and devotion by accepting her half eaten fruit and eating it lovingly. Love, faith, joy and devotion make for a very healthy recipe for radiance.

The idea of this book had been fermenting in the vessel of my mind for too long and I realized that it was time to tell the story, for in the telling of this story would the taste of pickle of my experiences be judged. Gently guided by Ayurvedic principles, and my study of modern nutrition and self-care theories; I decided to present to you recipes that have given me satiation and pleasure. Ayurveda suggests that if all the six taste buds are satisfied during a meal, you do not crave unhealthy junk food. The food recipes in this book satisfy all the six tastes of sweet, sour, pungent, astringent, salty and bitter.

Following simple guidelines regarding diet and adhering to an organic way of living, helps us to nurture our body and brings balance. A very significant guideline to follow regarding diet is to look at our traditional diet. Joshua Rosenthal, Robert and Melanie Sachs, recommend going back to our roots and eating what we ate as a child. Quite often, the secrets to our good health lies in connecting with our inner child and finding what gave us joy.

Sometimes the food we ate as a child may not be the healthiest, but a little of that connects us with our spirit and ignites a sense of joy and this further leads to satiation or satisfaction with just a little amount. You will find that two handfuls of food are enough at a meal time, if you are eating in a happy and joyous frame of mind. Some simple guidelines about diet are listed here; easy to follow they assist the body in effectively ingesting, digesting and eliminating.

Always invoke the Universe to assist you in the preparation of food, cook with a happy frame of mind and make sure you sit and eat in a clean tidy environment. Choose organic fresh ingredients and eat freshly cooked meals. Sit peacefully when you are ready to eat and offer a prayer or grace. It is best not to talk while you eat. Eat slowly and chew well each mouthful to release the enzymes and to feel more satiated. Eat in a timely manner every day and keep a gap of few hours between meals, unless you are a diabetic; this assists in the proper digestion of the food. Avoid cold water while eating as this will inhibit proper digestion. Drink water twenty minutes before a meal, then wait for twenty minutes after the meal and have a cup of warm water, this aids in the digestion process.

The recipes I have shared in this book are time tested and true, the measurements are approximate. I encourage you to cook from your spirit. The calories may not be concise in these recipes, but your spirit will be satiated with eating just a little. The ingredients are a mix of traditional and novel, also added are some suggestions for healthier choices. I have never measured to cook, a little bit of this and a little bit of that has been my motto, for both food and skincare recipes.

Experimenting and customizing whatever was the need of the day and keeping in mind the availability of fresh ingredients, you can create over one hundred and eight recipes with just the sauces and garam masala recipe given at the end of this chapter.

Take a vegetable of your choice, wash it, cut it into suitable pieces, sauté it in a little oil of your choice, add a spoonful of a cooking sauce of your choice from the recipes below, add spices and salt according to your taste. Stir and simmer until vegetable is cooked. Say a prayer or affirmation for good health and present it as an offering to yourself. Cook intuitively! It is that simple!

Purity of intentions, abundance of love, prayers while cooking, faith, joy, devotion and compassion are the ingredients common in all the recipes shared herein. Enjoy!

> *Food is much more than a bunch of chemicals.*
> *Food is energy and information*
> *– Mark David*

garam masalo

hot allspice mix

ingredients – *samagri* or *seedho*

4 tablespoons roasted cumin
4 tablespoons coriander seeds
3 tablespoons black peppercorns
1 stick cinnamon
1 teaspoon cloves
1 nutmeg
few bay leaves

method – *vidhi*

In a shallow saucepan, slowly dry roast the above mentioned spices. Stirring them often, make sure they do not burn. Once they emanate a warm spicy aroma, turn of the heat and let them cool. You may also toast these spices in an oven. Grind them in a dry grinder until finely powdered. Store in an airtight container and use as per your taste or the need of the recipe.

Do you think you can change the spices to suit the seasons? Why or why not? Pen your thoughts here and experiment, make your own *garam masalo*.

sao masalo

green garlic and mint sauce

ingredients – *samagri* or *seedho*

1 large bunch cilantro
1 medium bunch fresh green mint
1 medium bunch green onions
1 small bunch chives or green garlic
10 green chilies
10 peeled garlic cloves
1 inch peeled ginger
1 teaspoon oil
½ teaspoon vinegar

method – *vidhi*

Combine all the ingredients and blend them in a blender to a sauce consistency. Bottle it and store it in fridge. Use as needed to flavor various dishes. It can be stored in fridge for a week, provided you refrigerate it immediately after each use.

When in a pinch, I have converted this green sauce into quick green chutney by adding a pinch of salt, little brown sugar, *chat masala* and lemon juice.

A little, blended with olive oil makes great minty garlic salad dressing.

What other herbs do you think can be effectively used in this sauce? Experiment!

bhugal masalo

golden brown sauce

ingredients – *samagri* or *seedho*

3 cups chopped onions
1 cinnamon stick
2 large black cardamoms
4 small green cardamoms
4 cloves
2 tablespoons organic ghee or oil

method – *vidhi*

In a large thick bottomed saucepan, heat up the ghee or oil, sauté the onion in this oil until golden brown. Add all other ingredients. Add a little water if needed, stir it, cover and cook gently on low flame until onion is soft and mushy. After cooling it, store in an airtight container in the fridge, use as a brown sauce for your vegetables as needed. If used correctly and refrigerated immediately after each use, it can be refrigerated in the fridge for up to a week.

How would different onions taste in this sauce? Do you think there would be a variation in flavors? Try it!

tamatan ji pat

tangy tomato sauce

ingredients – *samagri* or *seedho*

3 cups chopped ripe tomatoes
1 inch piece of peeled ginger or ½ teaspoon of dried ginger or sundh
1 whole dried red chili
2 bay leaves
1 clove
2 green cardamoms
½ teaspoon onion seed or *basari ja bijh*
1 teaspoon organic ghee or oil of your choice

method – *vidhi*

In a blender, puree tomatoes and ginger. In a thick bottomed saucepan, heat the ghee or oil. Add all the dry spices, gently stir and gradually add the pureed tomatoes and ginger. Cook on medium heat until the sauce thickens a little. Remove from heat, cool and store in the fridge in an airtight container. Your Tamatan ji pat is ready to use as needed for various vegetable dishes that require tomato sauce. This can last for a week, if stored properly and refrigerated immediately after each use.

In a rush when I have need a sweet and sour chutney, I have added organic brown sugar, salt to taste and boiled the sauce little more to make a tasty tomato chutney. Adding maple syrup or agave nectar to the tomato sauce works equally well, to make tomato chutney.

A little, added to the olive oil makes a great tangy salad dressing. The possibilities are endless, I just love to experiment and play with the ingredients I have on my hand.

Do you think we can experiment some more? Go ahead, do it intuitively!

aesthetics....*saundarya*

Traditional Ayurveda fits quite well into modern models of holistic healing, concerned with a broad view of the total health of the individual: physically, emotionally, and spiritually. What Ayurveda offers to these models beyond its own techniques is a deeper awareness of how the body and our experiences are a microcosm of the greater universe and the relationships in the interaction between our inner and outer worlds
– Melanie Sachs

Our skin speaks and has many stories to tell, if only we would listen. Our happiness, joy, love, grace and radiance is reflected in our healthy skin, as is guilt, abuse, sadness and stress reflected in unhealthy skin. There are new secrets revealed everyday by our skin, as it changes. It reflects our illness by becoming dry, cracked or distressed. When we are in perfect health, it radiates a healthy glow. The largest organ of our body, it presents the world with our external beauty along with protecting the internal organs.

This integumentary system is a living system that also comprises of hair, nails, glands and various receptors. It protects us from physical, chemical, biological, thermal and electrical aggression. It acts as a moisture regulator and barrier, by preventing loss of moisture or excessive entry. It serves as sensitive sensory organ, responding to heat, cold, pain, pleasure and pressure. It helps our body to maintain a steady temperature preventing excessive loss of moisture and minerals. It metabolizes and stores fat; converts ultra violet rays into Vitamin D3, assisting in the healthy absorption of calcium and other minerals necessary for strong bones. It secretes sebum, and assists in process of excretion of salts, urea, water and toxins via sweating. It constantly transmits and receives information.

Mainly our skin comprises of three layer, epidermis, dermis and subcutaneous or adipose tissue. Home to melanocytes, epidermis the outermost layer is responsible for the color and tone of our skin. Dermis or the dermal layer lies below the epidermis and is made up of elastic connective tissue. The two main components found in this layer are elastin and collagen, which are responsible for the elasticity and structure and for holding internal organs and bones together. The third layer of skin is the subcutaneous layer and it lies below the dermis storing the fat necessary for contour and smoothness; circulation is maintained here by network of arteries and lymphatic system.

As a skincare educator and a holistic health coach, I have always emphasized the importance of natural, organic ingredients in skincare regime and products. I remind health conscious seekers, who are into healthy detox to remember to use only pure organic ingredients on their skin as they detox their body. For if they are cleansing their internal organs by performing a detox, but applying skincare products loaded with chemicals and harsh ingredients, they are defeating the purpose of a successful detox. They are putting harsh toxins right back into their system, through their skin.

As the various stories from the mythology and facts from the folklores were shared with me by my elders, I learnt that Ayurveda was a 5,000-year-old system of natural healing had its origins in the Vedic culture of India. The three main Ayurvedic texts were the *Charaka Samhita, Sushruta Samhita* and the *Ashtanga Hridaya Samhita*. The Ashtanga Hridaya Samhita, written by *Vagbhatta* of Sind, serves as a framework for current Tibetan Ayurveda. Three lesser known texts of Ayurveda are *Sharngadhara Samhita, Bhava Prakasha*, and *Madhava Nidanam*. According to these texts *Lord Dhanwantri* is the discoverer or father of Ayurveda, and is considered the physician of the deities like the *Ashwini* and *Kumaras*.

I was reminded that although suppressed during the years of foreign occupation, Ayurveda had survived and emerged again in modern times. Ayurveda was the root that strengthened the branches of Tibetan and Traditional Chinese medicine. It is a well-known fact, that early Greek medicine also embraced many concepts originally expressed in the classical Ayurvedic texts.

Recognizing that human beings are part of the nature, Ayurveda describes three fundamental energies that govern our inner and outer environments; movement, transformation, and structure. Known in Sanskrit as *Vata* or Wind, *Pitta* or Fire, and *Kapha* or Earth, these primary forces are responsible for the characteristics of our mind and body. As I ran through the meadows playing in the wind, I noted that I was exhilarated and wound up on a hot summer day, if I played too much in the sun, I returned home flushed and irritated. On a lazy winter day, if I stayed cocooned inside without much activity I noted that I felt lethargic. As I noticed these subtle signals of the nature, I asked questions from my elders.

I learnt that for each element, there is a balanced and imbalanced expression. An important goal according to Ayurveda is to identify our ideal state of balance, determine where we are out of balance, and choose interventions using diet, herbs, aromatherapy, massage treatments, music, yoga and meditation to reestablish balance. Internal health and balance is what brings radiance to outer skin. In Ayurveda, soothing, purifying and nurturing pure herbs are mixed according to the constitution. These herbs are ingested as we continue the course of prescribed therapies; as well as used externally during a facial or the body treatment. An Ayurvedic facial and body treatments consists of different combinations of herbal ingredients and therapies like marma point massage, scalp massage, lymphatic drainage massage, breathing techniques, aromatherapy and hydrotherapy.

As children if we had high fever, the first thing Sugi did was gently rub our feet with raw goat milk early in the morning, before the sun rose. This would support in bringing down the fever without dehydrating us. *Tulsi Kada* or basil tea was made with basil leaves, spices and other herbs; and we were asked to sip that to help with colds. Warm milk with a pinch of turmeric before retiring at night was a normal practice especially during monsoons and winters.

A science of healing the self, Ayurveda encompasses nutrition and diet, skin and body care, rest and relaxation, breathing and meditation, medicinal and aromatic herbs, exercise and yoga, as well as rejuvenating and restoring practices for healing the whole being. It encourages us to go to the root of the cause, because symptoms are manifestations of imbalance at the root. Along with this it also recognizes the role of music, color, gems and metals in balancing of the mind, body and spirit.

Prakriti or our individual constitution is closely related to the modern scientific principle of the genetic code. As a massage therapist and an aesthetician I had always looked at the genetic predisposition of a client before customizing their treatment. Lessons in determining the *Prakriti* during the course of my Ayurvedic studies validated my reasoning for understanding a client as whole being. Although *Prakriti* remains constant, other outside factors keep changing. It is keeping in mind the effects of these changes; that we take responsibility for our own healing.

As a little girl I had watched my grandmother and aunts use various natural ingredients for their skin care regime. *Tail, tel* or oils were infused with herbs to treat various conditions. *Brahmi*, an herb that grew wildly in the meadows was often collected, washed and soaked in the oil overnight. It was brought to boil on low heat on the *sigri*, simmered and then cooled. Sometimes other herbs like *Rosemary* and *Ashwagandha* were added for different preparations. Different oils were prepared for different constitutions and seasons. Sesame oil, mustard oil, sunflower oil and coconut oil were most commonly used in these preparations.

Cleansers and exfoliants were made with simple chick pea powder and herbs. Depending on the skin condition, for instance lemon was used with chick pea powder and turmeric for oily skin, where as fresh cream and turmeric was used for dry skin.

Yoghurt, *Ghee* and *Multani Mitti* or fullers earth was always was readily available in every home to use as a mask base. We played with various flower petals, fruits, vegetables and herbs from our own gardens and experimented with new recipes for skin care. We would rub leftover lemon peel on our knees and elbows because we knew that it would brighten them. Closing our eyes we would squeeze the orange peel and spritz it on our face and know that it would tone our skin.

Fresh *Henna* leaves were picked from *Henna* or *Mehndi* bushes and ground into a paste to make various designs to decorate our hands and feet. This paste was also used for cooling the inflammation of cracked heels and blistered toes. A natural dye for hair, *Henna* was also used along with, tea leaves, lemon juice and other healing herbs for coloring and conditioning of the dark hair.

When using herbs and essential oils, special caution was applied if a woman was pregnant or nursing. They were restricted from using some stimulating ingredients like *Chandan* or Sandalwood. *Panchakarma* or detoxification was never recommended for menstruating, pregnant or lactating women.

Champi or Scalp massages, *Abhyanga* or body massage, *Padabhyanga* or foot treatment, were all performed at home with simple tools like silk or cotton gloves, pumice stones and *kansa vatis* or metal bowls. As we massaged our scalp, arms and feet; with warm oils, infusions and poultices; we learnt the art of self-nurture.

At the time of her wedding a traditional Hindu bride is adorned with sixteen adornments or *Solah Shingaar*. Each adornment is used for a particular reason, as is the beautification process which starts several days before the wedding. She is receives daily oil massages, using herbs that strengthen her reproductive organs and bring calmness during a stressful time. Women in the family apply a fragrant paste made of sandalwood and turmeric, all over her body. This is said to purify and calm her skin while centering her mind, additionally it brings a gentle glow to her skin. Many such beauty enhancing rituals were performed using various grains, ghee, oils, herbs and spices. There was a reason for using turmeric, basil, sandalwood on such occasion, as these ingredients had anti-inflammatory, oxygenating, purifying and balancing properties which worked well during stressful long rituals.

Each ornament she is adorned with has significance and balances her energy centers. Starting with *Kum Kum* or the red adornment on the forehead, *Sindoor* or vermilion powder lining the mid hairline, *Kajal* or the kohl, *Attar* or the perfume, *Mehndi* or the Henna, *Gajra* or the floral garland, *Mattha Patti* or the jewelry adorning the hairline, *Nath* or the nose ring, *Karn Phool* or the earrings, *Kanth Haar* or the necklace, *Mangal Sutra* a onyx or coral bead *mala* for protection, *Chooriyan* or the bangles, *Anghooti* or rings, *Kamar Patti* or the waist band, *Payal* or the anklets and *Bichua* or the toe rings; each is significantly worn on the body to touch an energy point, bringing balance. Made from the purest herbs, spices, flowers, gems and metals, these adornments are sanctified with prayers for a happy married life.

Living in harmony with the rhythms' of nature was always encouraged. Food was cooked and consumed according to *Ritu* or seasons in a timely manner. So also our skin consumed nourishing ingredients according to the changing seasons. Internal balance was supported with external nourishment. A daily routine or *Dincharaya* was observed. This was considered as essential for maintaining good health and improved functioning of our body, mind and spirit. It established balance and regulated the biological functions. Generating discipline, harmony, joy and longevity, it promoted proper assimilation and absorption of the vital nutrients.

During a period of illness, as I decided to revert to my roots; I embraced the modern approach to Ayurveda. Learning from Robert and Melanie Sachs, Bri. Maya Tiwari, Dr. John Douillard, Dr. Vasant Lad, Dr. David Simon and Dr. Deepak Chopra, helped me realize that more than just a system of treating illness, Ayurveda is a science of life. Simply explained, *Ayur* means life, *Veda* means science or knowledge. It offers a body of wisdom designed to help us stay vital while realizing our full potential. Providing guidelines on ideal daily and seasonal routines, diet, behavior, temperament and the proper use of our senses, Ayurveda reminds us that health is the balanced integration between our environment, mind, body and spirit.

The first step I learnt on this transformative journey was to understand my *Dosha* or imbalances and take responsibility for my own health. Once we accept our imperfections and ailments we are ready to take a step towards balance and perfecting of health. Realizing that our health depends on our realization of self, Ayurveda expounds on the theory that in order to unite with our creator, we need to unite with our self. The four governing, fundamental *Pursharthas,* of *Dharma* or duty, *Artha* or prosperity, *Kama* or healthy desires and *Moksha* or liberation can only be attained by healthy body, mind and spirit in balance. If we are in imbalance we cannot fulfil our duty or right actions, if we cannot do our work well then prosperity and abundance eludes us. Our healthy or positive desires propel us towards harmony and balance of mind, body and spirit. I embarked on the journey of self-care by making simple lifestyle changes.

Establishing *Dincharaya* or a disciplined daily routine was not easy in this hectic lifestyle I was leading, but gradually I embraced it more wholeheartedly as I saw healthy results.

These basic *Dincharaya* or daily ritual principles have helped me improve my health and are simple and uncomplicated. My daily routine comprises of my waking up in a timely manner before sunrise, saying a prayer of gratitude, washing my face and eyes, drinking a glass of water, elimination, cleaning my tongue and teeth, gargling, and application of *Nasya* and performing self *Abhyanga*. As I wait for the oils to be absorbed, I exercise gently stretching my body. This is followed by a shower, prayers and meditation. I then write in my journal and list ten blessings of the day. All this is usually accomplished within an hour.

At this time I sit down and enjoy my breakfast and then prepare for the day, starting my slow cooker so my dinner is ready when I arrive home in the evening. Lunch is usually eaten at work; I tend to carry a large salad or soup and sometimes food left over from the previous night's dinner. Upon return in the evening we have a glass of freshly made juice and leave for a walk. Preceded by a quick shower, dinner is usually between six thirty and seven pm. As I do the dishes I chant and sing and my children now follow the same practices. We stay as positive and cheerful as possible avoiding any TV news and programs, especially at night. I love to read and before our children moved away due to marriage and their jobs, we used to read a passage from scriptures and self-improvement books, discussing the essence of their teachings.

Receiving a massage from the skilled hands of a therapist is of course a preferred choice to relax, but you can learn to perform these various therapies at home for daily home care. I pour a little oil in my cupped palm, dip my index and middle fingers into the oil and pour a few drops of oil on three points on my mid hairline. Rubbing the rest of the oil between my hands, I run my hands through my hair. Massaging my scalp with my fingertips in a circular motion, I move on to my ears massaging them gently. Holding a few strands of my hair in my hands I gently tug at them, increasing the circulation. I end this with gentle tapotement with my fingers and gently run my hands through oil covered hair.

A simple face massage routine helps me to sleep better and aids with circulation and the release of facial tension. Starting at my forehead, I gently stoke my face with outward motion, starting from the center, covering the forehead, cheeks and chin area. Sweeping from the center of my forehead I gently pinch my eyebrows moving towards my temple. Repeating three times, I gently press thrice at my temples. Placing my index fingers under my lip and thumbs under my chin, I gently press and release sweeping along the jawbone until I reach my ears. Gently massaging my ears, both front and behind, I stop at my temples gently pressing three times. Rubbing my hands and cupping them gently over my eyes and cheeks, I lift my cheeks gently with my cupped hands and release. This stimulates nerves controlling the facial muscles and relaxes and tones the face. I end this massage by gently tapping under the chin and stroking my décolleté with outward motion from the center.

For a full body self *Abhyanga*, I continue by moving from the décolleté, going towards the shoulders, gently massaging both left and right shoulder joints. I usually do this practice while standing in a bath tub. Always keeping in mind to move towards the heart, I then massage my arms and hands in an upsweep manner, gently stroking and rotating each finger. From the base of my ribs and sternum, I bring my hand up to the right side and then repeat this on left side.

Using gentle circular motion, I massage my abdomen clockwise. Alternating with both hands, from below the rib cage, I massage the abdomen to the top of the pubis bone. Sitting on the edge of the tub, I lift one foot on to my knee, gently massaging my feet, rotating the ankle joint and each toe; repeating this on the other foot as well. Lowering my legs, I massage them in an upward motion, gently massaging the calves and knee joints, moving up to my thighs. I then reach up as high as I can on my lower back and gently massage my lower back, with upward brisk strokes. Gently placing my hands in a prayer position, I thank my body for its strength and good health.

The ingredients I use are natural and organic. I believe that our body recognizes these ingredients easily as we have ingested them in some fashion or form. I look at nature for answers and follow a *Ritucharya* or a seasonal routine. As the weather changes so do the ingredients in my food and skin care products.

Nature gives us subtle signals, we just need to be observant and pay attention. I remember playing with various vegetables and nuts and sharing the experience with my children in a playful manner as they grew. When eating walnuts, we would crack them open and gleefully compare it to a brain. Tomatoes when halved presented chambers of the heart and Lycopene I explained to them was a *Rasa* or an essence of tomatoes and was great for supporting heart health. Carrots when sliced depicted the shape of iris, and are known to support our eye health.

As I retire for the evening, I usually sponge my body with a wash cloth paying especial attention to my face, hands and feet. I say a prayer of gratitude before retiring for the day. These skin and body care rituals and recipes which follow, have taught me to reconnect with myself. They have taught me the joyous acceptance of my physical body, as I wholeheartedly embraced my perfections and imperfections. As I touch each part of my body, I revel in the marvelous discovery of hitherto neglected beauty residing in my being. I hope that an introduction to these recipes and rituals transports you to the delightful realms of self-discovery, leading you further to the joys of self-nurture.

> *There is beauty to be found in the changing of the earth's seasons, and an inner grace in honoring the cycles of life*
> *– Jack Kornfield*

ubtan or cleansers and exfoliants

Ubtan or cleanser and exfoliants, help cleanse our face and body gently. Various herbs and spices are combined with legume or chick pea powder, keeping in mind the skin and body constitution or *Prakriti and doshas*.

basic tridoshic ubtan

ingredients – *samagri*

4 tablespoon chick pea powder or *Besan*
1 tablespoon organic almond or sesame oil, milk or honey
½ teaspoon powdered fuller's earth or bentonite clay
1/4 teaspoon each of ground or powdered herbal ingredients of choice like dried basil, turmeric, mint, rose, neem and triphala

method – *vidhi*

Blend the chick pea powder, fuller's earth, turmeric, neem, mint, basil and triphala with honey, milk or oil. You may add a little water if needed. Make a paste and apply all over the face, avoiding eye and lip area. Allow it to dry and set for ten minutes, gently removing in an upward sweep. Remove excess with a wash cloth and tepid water. You can powder the dry ingredients and store them in an airtight container, for later use.

oils or moisturizers

Oil, *Tail* or *Tel* is used in massage or *Abhyanga* to soothe and stabilize the face and body. It also acts as carriers for nourishing herbs and aromas, which bring balance to body. A wide variety of oils like sweet almond, sunflower, jojoba, avocado and apricot are used for massaging, however, sesame oil is found to be the most effective in *Abhyanga*.

Essential oils and herbs that are suitable for dry, cool *Vata* skin are Rose, Rose Geranium, Rosewood and Neroli, while reactive, hot *Pitta* responds well to Lemon, Jasmine, Bergamont and Frankincense; heavy, moist, cold *Kapha* does well with Orange, Rosemary, Juniper and Bergamont.

In addition to just these few ingredients you can create over one hundred and eight recipes for radiance by using various different oils, herbs, flowers, essential oils and spices.

herbal oil decoction

ingredients – *samagri*

6 cups water
1 1/2 cups oil
1/8 cup herbs of choice

method – *vidhi*

Boil water in a thick bottomed stainless steel pot. Add oil and herbs, cover and simmer on low heat for 6 to 8 hours, or until the water has evaporated. Allow the oil to cool, and then pour oil through a muslin cloth into a glass or earthen jar and store in a cool place.

herbal oil infusion

ingredients – *samagri*

2 cups oil
½ cup herbs of choice

method – *vidhi*

Boil oil in a thick bottomed stainless steel pot. Add herbs and remove from heat. Cover and let it seep overnight. Strain through muslin cloth into an earthen or glass jar. Store it in a cool, dry place.

rituals and regimes

Since many thousand years, these rituals have been the recipes for balance, nourishment, good health and radiance. The fact that these ingredients, rituals and recipes have lasted for this long and survived the test of time tell us that they actually work and are an efficacious way of bringing our mind, body and spirit into balance. A note of caution here though, it is recommended that if you are trying to be pregnant, pregnant, lactating or menstruating; kindly consult with your aesthetician, Ayurvedic practitioner or healthcare provider before trying any new recipes or rituals.

abhyanga

A full body massage with warm oils, Abhyanga is designed to improve the circulation, decrease dryness and combat the problems associated with aging. It is a very relaxing massage performed by one or multiple therapists. There are various forms of Abhyanga performed for various ages and body types.

Shishu Abhyanga is a very gentle and nurturing full body massage of an infant, performed from birth until the age of two. It is traditionally performed at home before bath, by the mother or grandmothers.

Soothika Abhyanga or the post natal massage is a very therapeutic and beneficial massage sequence performed on postnatal women for forty days after delivery. This brings balance to internal organs, strengthening and toning the muscles.

Shiroabhyanga or a traditional scalp massage usually performed at home; has become a popular spa treatment now. *Champi* as it is known in spa treatments relaxes the muscles of neck and face, improving the circulation and toning the facial muscles.

Vishesh is a specialized invigorating deep tissue massage with warm medicated herbal oils. It revitalizes and stimulates the immune system; aiding in removing tension in the muscles and connective tissues.

marma chikitsa

Marma Chikitsa or simply put the *Marma* point massage is a gentle pressing, touching or rubbing of vital energy centers; this therapy assists in natural healing process of the body.

Kalari is a martial art practiced in Kerala. It is also known as the *Padagaaatha* or massage by feet. A highly skilled therapist manipulates the body with feet, activating the *Marmas* or the pressure points in the body. This is said to be beneficial and encourages the energy flow.

padabhyanga

Padabhyanga is a rejuvenating foot massage; it relaxes the whole body by stimulating the nerve centers in the feet.

Kansa Vataki, a very specialized technique, *Kansa* metal bowls are used to massage the soles of the feet to bring balance in the body. *Kansa* is a formulation of three precious metals and helps in relieving of tension and relaxing of the body.

udvartana

Udvartana is a stimulating and exfoliating massage performed with herbal pastes or powders. It assists in proper cleansing, exfoliation and stimulation of the lymphatic system.

Grashana a dry brushing massage performed with silk or wool gloves is a stimulating massage which supports the circulation and balancing of acidity in the body.

lepana

A simple but deeply therapeutic application of herbal compresses and poultices; *Lepana*, assists in reducing inflammation and swelling. Clays and muds of different nature are also used in this therapy to draw out the toxins.

Pishinchali is a vigorous full body massage performed to mobilize the muscles and ligaments of the body. Small bags filled with an infusion of cooked rice and herbs are used along with dosha specific warm oils.

swedana

There are various types of steam and heat treatments used in Ayurvedic therapy.

Tapa Swedana or an application of dry heat helps to reduce inflammation in the joints and is a very therapeutic treatment.

Bhaspa Swedana a gentle steam bath for full body is designed to mobilize the toxins in the skin and deeper tissues. Caution must be observed while you sit in a steam cabinet to keep your head out and heart and genitals be covered with cool damp towels.

Drava Swedana is a warm herbal bath that is given before full body massage.

In *Nadi Swedana* a localized steam is applied to specific parts of body like large joints to ease the tension, pain and improve the range of motion. This is usually performed as a part of the *Purva karma* therapy, during *Panchakarma*.

purva karma

Purva Karma is a series of oil massages, usually performed before *Panchakarma*. All the toxins are brought into the gut and then eliminated through the *Panchakarma* therapy.

panchakarama

Panchakarma is a five-fold purification treatment, for rejuvenating the body. Enemas, laxatives, therapeutic vomiting, nasal cleansing, is performed under the care of a licensed physician. It is a process which starts with using various techniques to bring the toxins to the gut, and then under a carefully watchful and supportive manner, eliminated from the body.

gandoosh

Ayurvedic oil pulling has gained a lot of popularity these days. In this very simple therapy, about a tablespoon of oil is held in the mouth, first thing in the morning before brushing your teeth. This is swished around the mouth just like a mouthwash for a few minutes without swallowing and is than spit out. This according to Ayurveda supports in strengthening the gums and teeth. You may increase the time up to twenty minutes once you have learned to do it correctly and efficiently.

raktamoksha

Raktamoksha literally means blood-letting. It is performed as a part of *Panchakarma* treatment and supports in refinement of blood. It supports in the elimination of the toxins from the blood stream though gastrointestinal tract and is considered as safe, painless and very effective therapy.

neti

Neti is the cleansing of the nasal passages of allergens and helps soothe the sinuses. A warm saline solution is used to irrigate the nasal passages.

nasya

Nasya is a nasal application of herbal oils. In this therapy oil is administered gently into nose. This helps in relieving of sinus pressure and helps with dark circles around the eyes.

netra basti

Netra Basti is an eye soothing therapy that supports in relaxation of eyes. Herbally infused ghee is used for various eye issues; for bathing the eyes.

karna purti

In the *Karna Purti* treatment, warm oil is applied to the ears to help relieve the jaw tension and ringing in the ears. These are usually done at different stages during the course of a *Panchakarma* treatment.

chakras

Our *Chakras* are the subtle energy centers of our body. Working with these energy centers, the whole body, mind and spirit can be brought to balance.

rattan

Gem therapy is the use of precious and semi-precious stones on the face and body to enhance the energy balance and mental clarity. Ayurvedic gem therapy suggests that each gem has specific property that helps specific doshas or constitutions and supports in bringing balance. It is believed that *Jyotish* and *Rattan* therapy make a very powerful combination for bringing balance in the energy field. Finely powdered gold, silver and pearls were known to be used in skincare preparations to enhance clarity and radiance.

mudra

Mudra is commonly associated with the hand gestures. Our fingers are related to different types of energies and when they are brought together in a specific manner they move subtle energies in our body. They help balance the flow of energy through the nadis that nourish our various internal and external organs. They also assist in mood elevation and aid in meditation.

nrithya

Dance therapy is found to be helpful in strengthening the bone structure and ligaments. It stimulates the cardiovascular system by increasing the heart rate. The body becomes supple and our mind becomes calm thus integrating mind, body and spirit.

naada

Music is a universal language which influences all levels of human existence. *Ragas* form the basis of a melody. Various *Ragas* have been found to be very effective in aiding in relaxation of mind, body and spirit.

dhyaan

Meditation or *Dhyaan* is an extended period of thought or contemplation, which leads to physical and mental stillness.

pranayama

Pranayama or correct breathing technique assists body to repose, restore and rejuvenate. Volumes have been written about this rejuvenating practice of correct breathing.

yoga

The word *Yoga* comes from a Sanskrit word which means to join or to unite. It is method of joining mind body and spirit, through various practices and exercises. Yoga is not a religion; it is a way of promoting self-awareness and balance and was developed independently as a system of philosophy by Patanjali, author of the old text book, the *yoga sutra*.

jyotish

Ayurvedic astrology is a comprehensive system of astrological interpretation, containing accurate methods for examining all aspects of human life from health to enlightenment. Also called *Jyotish*, it is the traditional astrology of India and part of greater system of yogic knowledge.

vastu

Vastu Shastra is an ancient science which deals with the Hindu view about how the laws of planets and nature affect human dwellings. These designs are based on integrating architecture with nature and ancient Indian beliefs utilizing *Yantra* or perfect geometric pattern, symmetry and directional alignments.

shirodhara

Shirodhara a gentle soothing therapy in which warm oils or herbal infusions are gently poured over the forehead; is a deeply relaxation treatment that is very helpful in reducing mental stress. The word *Shiro* means head and *dhara* means a gentle stream. The liquids usually used in Shirodhara depend on the constitution or the *Prakriti*; they include warm oil, milk, buttermilk, coconut water and sometimes just herbal water.

kaya kalpa

Kaya Kalpa is a totally transforming therapy. An ancient rejuvenating and restoring treatment procedure, *Kaya Kalpa* is performed as a solitary retreat for varying periods of time. It is a powerful combination of *Ayurveda*, *Yoga*, and *Meditation* which is said to restore youthfulness, agility and radiance.

deontology....*acharan rasayana*

You are like a human transmission tower, transmitting a frequency with your thoughts. If you want to change anything in your life, change the frequency by changing your thoughts
— Rhonda Byrne

Radiance, a quality of brightness and happiness that can be seen on a person's face, is also a warm, soft light that shines from within. According to *Yajurveda*, attractiveness and magnetism of a man's personality is the result of his inner radiance.

Churned into the nectar of previous and following chapters are my favorite food recipes as well as skin and body care recipes and rituals. As I tried to heal my body through healthy diet and self-nurture; I realized that there was still a missing piece of the puzzle. Upon deeper introspection, I started noting a connection between my emotions and diet and was reminded of lessons learnt in childhood. Holding on to the stressful pattern of the pain from my past, I had been finding comfort in self-neglect. As I consciously checked my emotions, I realized that the best organic foods and lifestyle changes were not doing their optimum job, because there was an emotional disconnect.

Once I found the missing piece of the puzzle I started becoming more mindful of my emotions, my thoughts, my words and my deeds. As I studied the philosophy of the law of attraction, I recognized the need to let go of the old patterns held in my mind, body and spirit.

Acharan Rasayana or application of positive thoughts and conduct is a very important part of *Charaka Samhita*. It reminds us to be mindful of our emotions and aware of our desires, for from the desires come the feelings and from feelings come thoughts. These thoughts lead us to actions, which in turn leads us to habits. Understanding this pattern of our desires and our reactions to its fulfilment or denial is to know our *Karma*. As we understand this we come closer to our *Karma*.

In Ayurveda knowing your body type is of fundamental importance, but not many understand that there are actually three different kind of body types to be aware of. While two of them are based on doshas of *vata, pitta* and *kapha* the third describes your mind and emotions.

The first body type *Karma Prakriti* or the birth body type, is what is best described as our innate nature. This body type is actually determined at conception, and represents our genetic makeup as passed down from our parents and even ancestors. This constitution also carries the mental and emotional factors that were carried by our parents during their lives up until the point of our conception.

It is known or referred to as the *Karmic* body type because it gives us the opportunity to act on our free will and relieve ourselves from old *Karmic* mental and emotional patterns which we bring to our life. Ayurveda believes in restoring balance and thus expressing and experiencing our own true nature. Understanding our birth body type is a lifelong study of self-inquiry and self-awareness geared towards attaining self-realization. But before we actually do that, we must bring our current body into balance.

The second body type is called the current body type, or *Deh Prakriti*. This is an assessment of our current lifestyle and all that has influenced us since our birth. It reflects physical, mental and the emotional qualities that have manifested as a result of influences in our lifetime. Understanding our *Deh Prakriti* offers us the opportunity to take action to free our self from old inhibiting mental and emotional designs, as well as physical imbalances that we have usually collected over a period of time.

The third body type is our mental constitution, which includes the emotional and even spiritual state of the mind. This is called the *Manas* or *Mano Prakriti*. This type is best described in terms of the three mental governing principles called *Sattvic, Rajasic* and *Tamasic*. *Sattvic* is that state of mind that is filled with love, compassion and contentment. *Rajasic* is that state of mind wherein it requires sense stimulation in order to experience contentment. *Tamasic* is when the mind dulls and retreats into extreme behavior of lethargy or aggravation.

According to Ayurveda, it is these self-inflicted patterns that eat at our body, our gut, and initiate the degenerative, aging and disease processes. The reason we need to be aware of these body types is to experience a greater sense of self-awareness, so we are not deceived by the illusion of patterns of behavior that have been imbibed by us since our childhood.

Further studies revealed that the emotions that affect our mind relate to the five basic elements; three *Doshas* or humors, three *Gunnas* or quality, the seven *Dhatus* or elements, the five senses, and *Prana* or vital life force. This leads us to the exploration of the field of *Rasa*.

The word for taste in Sanskrit is *Rasa*. *Rasa* also means nectar, as in essence of life in a plant and the essence of life in us. Most accurately, *Rasa* also refers to our feelings and sentiments, referring to the nine emotions experienced by us; *Shringara* or love and beauty, *Hasya* or joy, *Adhbhuta* or wonder, *Veera* or courage, *Shanta* or peace, *Karuna* or compassion, *Rudra* or anger, *Bhaya* or fear, *Vibhatsa* or disgust. As we can see, the single word *Rasa* has a wide range of meanings, all of which are interconnected.

From the Ayurvedic point of view, internal disharmony, lack of joy or *Nirasta* is caused by the lack of coordination of individuals' senses, emotions, thoughts and feelings. It is this lack of ability to process thoughts in a suitable manner, which leads to undigested emotions. Some of us are able to let go and move on easily, others slowly process their thoughts which often leaves a residue of negative impressions. When we triumph over our negative emotions by accepting them for what they are, we invite the *Sattva* or the positive energy into our life. The process of inviting *Sattva* or positive and pure qualities into our life is simple.

Once this connection was made, my health made a rapid turnaround. A people pleaser, I learnt to politely say no to others and hence yes to myself. It was not easy, as many feathers were ruffled and many unpleasant moments ensued, but gradually people who truly cared, understood my reasoning and stayed close. As I practiced self-appreciation, self-love; I gave permission to those around me to do the same.

As I remembered the cheerful surrender of Sugi to the developments in her life, I learnt to reconnect with my bliss. I once again retraced my steps to my childhood and learnt to live in complete faith and trust. Knowing that all is well, I learnt to rejoice in the present moment. I needed to take some essential steps and these are the steps I share with you now.

I have learned to listen to my body's needs by paying undivided attention during self-massage or *Abhyanga* and *Dhyaan* or meditation. Just ten minutes of being mindful and attentive during self *abhyanga* brings rich dividends. By touching each part of my body, I acknowledge its value and importance. As I touch each part I affirm that all is well and my body is a beautiful temple that houses my soul or spirit. I thank my eyes for showing me beautiful sights, I thank my nose for breathing pure air, leading up to my feet, which I thank for bearing my weight, carrying me through life and connecting me with the energy of mother earth. I express gratitude to each part and organ of my body and to the universe for residing within it.

When I started to believe that I am healthy, I became healthy.

Jagrukta or mindfulness was an important lesson in this process. Mindfulness is the intentional, accepting and non-judgmental focus of one's attention on the emotions, thought and sensations occurring in the present given moment. The more mindful I became of my surroundings, my ambience, my food, my skincare and my intentions; easier the path to self- healing became.

This I was able to do primarily through *Dhyaan* or meditation, According to *Mukunda Upanishad*, one who meditates, opens all the knots of his heart, all his bondages are opened; all his doubts are eliminated and he becomes gradually free from the fetters of actions and reactions. Simply put meditation is a practice in which an individual calms the mind, to realize some stress reducing benefit or as an end itself.

The prelude to this was my practice of *Prathana* or prayers. Prayers for me is my way of connecting with the source, universe or God within me and asking a question. In mediation I receive the answer through this practice of mindfulness. Interconnected, interwoven these three led me to making better choices.

Satsang is a spiritual congregation of likeminded souls who come together to pray, meditate and chant. In doing, so they not only raise their own vibration, but also that of their home and the community they live in. Simply put, it is spiritual socializing with congregation of our choosing. It could be in a Temple, at a Church, at a *Dargah*, at a *Gurudwara*, at a meditation center or in our own home.

I have incorporated several of these practices in my *Dincharaya* or daily routine. I realized that these positive practices and affirmations if practiced daily, lead to a balance in mind, body and spirit.

The *Satvikta, Pavitrata* or the purity of my diet was enhanced by my practice of mindfulness as it added another dimension to my eating experience. I was chewing more and enjoying various flavors as they caressed my tongue and satisfied my hunger. I became satiated more easily. My digestion improved and so did elimination.

Mindful *Pranayama* eased the tension in my physical body and relaxed my mind and body. Correct breathing freed up a lot of anxiety and calmed my mind.

As I regained my strength, I started indulging in *Kundalini Yoga* as this I found this to be the gentlest of the yoga practices. Through gentle stretching and soulful chanting of the *Mool Mantra*, I once again reconnected with Sugi's spiritual practices. The chants were not foreign to me as I had been reciting them since I was a little girl.

My study of *Adhmiyakta* or spirituality and *Manochintan* or contemplation gently guided me to experiencing and analyzing the feelings of *Hersh* or joy, *Abhaar* or gratitude, *Anukampa* or kindness, *Bhakti* or devotion, *Vinamrata* or humility and *Santosh* or contentment.

Through the simple application of *Prathana* or prayer, *Dhairya* or patience and *Dhrrta* or perseverance, I was beginning to enhance the quality of my life.

As the *Nav Rasa* or nine essences of *Shringara* or love and beauty, *Hasya* or joy, *Adhbhuta* or wonder, *Veera* or courage, *Shanta* or peace, *Karuna* or compassion, *Rudra* or anger, *Bhaya* or fear, *Vibhatsa* or disgust started flooding my mind, body and spirit; I was able to distinguish them clearly and accept them by connecting with the dark and the light side of the emotions. Acknowledging and accepting the good and the bad in life filled me with *Parmananda* or Bliss.

The reason I have emphasized the use of the positive words in this chapter, is to reaffirm that the conscious use of positive words leads to positive thinking and conduct. Our words may be light on our lips, but carry a weight and impact that is exceedingly valuable. Simply put, this is the reason that various *Mantras* harness our breath and transport us to the higher consciousness, during our meditation practice.

So when we choose an organic diet and organic skincare routine, we also need to complement it with mindful or conscious adherence to organic words, thoughts and actions.

As we ingest our food through our mouth, and skincare through our skin, so also we ingest positive words through our ears and feel them in our heart. The digestion process for our food happens in our gut, which has feelings just like our heart. The skincare that we ingest through skin also gets processed in our blood stream which passes through our heart for purification. As we process the nutrients from the food and skincare, so do we process positive words, thoughts and actions through our mind.

When all three are processed with juices of joy and love the end results are a healthy, happy and wise body, mind and spirit. This is where the *Satchidanand* or true heartfelt bliss resides and this is the true recipe for radiance.

Following are some uplifting positive affirmative words and quotes for unveiling your pure essence and radiance. You may choose your own, and that is fine. Just pick one positive word a day and contemplate on it for just a few minutes and see what it brings up for you, then journal your thoughts.

> *The thoughts I chose to think and believe right now are creating my future. These thoughts form my experiences tomorrow, next week and next year*
> *– Louise Hay*

uplift....*utthaan*

Here is a collection of some empowering words to begin your journaling with. I have also given the Hindi translation of the words and some meaningful quotes to set you thinking. These authors have shaped our thinking and inspired us with their words. Look at a quote with a different set of eyes, the words herein are the ingredients and thought itself is a recipe for radiance. Choose the ingredients of your words mindfully today, for they are creating your recipe for radiance for tomorrow. Radiance also comes from alignment of your thoughts and actions.

Love: *Prema*

If you judge people you have no time to love them – Mother Teresa

Joy: *Hersh*

When you are alive with joy, gratitude and genuine interest in others, you are your most beautiful – Brendon Burchard

Peace: *Shanti*

God, make me a hollow reed speak through me and let me be an instrument of peace – Anna Taylor

Abundance: *Prachurta*

One key to abundance in every area of life is this: we experience God's peace and harmony to the extent that we love, forgive, and focuses on the good in others and ourselves – Marianne Williamson

Action: *Anuyojan*

When we cast our bread upon water, we can presume that someone downstream whose face we may never see will benefit from our actions – Maya Angelou

Gratitude: *Abhaar*

And still after all this time, the sun never said to earth "you owe me". Look what happens with love like that – Rumi

Mindfulness: *Jagrukta*

The most precious gift we can offer anyone is our attention. When mindfulness embraces those we love, they will bloom like flowers – Thich Nhat Hanh

Compassion: *Krupa*

If your compassion does not include yourself, it is incomplete – Buddha

Grace: *Anugrah*

The winds of grace are always blowing, but you have to raise the sail – Sri Ramakrishna Paramhansa

Kindness: *Anukampa*

A single act of kindness throws out roots in all directions. And the roots spring up and make new trees – Amelia Earhart

Faith: *Vishwas*

Faith is the bird that feels the light and sings when the dawn is still dark – Rabindranath Tagore

Happy: *Khush*

Ever since happiness heard your name, it has been running through the streets trying to find you – Hafiz

Blossom: *Viksit*

May all that is unlived in you blossom into a future graced with love – John O'Donohue

Inspire: *Prerit*

I am here to serve. I am here to inspire. I am here to love. I am here to live my truth – Dr. Deepak Chopra

Dance: *Nrithya*

And those who were seen dancing were thought to be insane by those who could not hear the music – Nietzsche

Uplift: *Utthaan*

The key is to keep company only with people who uplift you, whose presence call forth your best - Epictetus

Praise: *Sarahana*

When you enter His presence with praise, He enters your circumstances with power – Joel Osteen

Enlighten: *Jyotirman*

There are many paths to enlightenment. Be sure to take the one with a heart – Lao Tzu

Rejoice: *Anandit*

This is the day the Lord hath made Rejoice! And be glad in it – Psalm 118:24

Amaze: *Vismit*

Our goal should be to live life in radical amazement...get up in the morning and look at the world in a way that takes nothing for granted. Everything is phenomenal; everything is incredible; never treat life casually. To be spiritual is to be amazed –Abraham Joshua Heschel

Vibrant: *Jivant*

When you have the courage to change your beliefs and behaviors so that you speak your truth and dare to cultivate pleasure instead of stress, you have the power to create a life of unbridled joy, unlimited abundance, and vibrant health – Dr. Christiane Northrup

Wisdom: *Gyan*

Turn your wounds into wisdom – Oprah Winfrey

Zest: *Utsah*

If you have zest and enthusiasm you attract zest and enthusiasm. Life does give back in kind – Norman Vincent Peale

Zeal: *Sagarmi*

Zeal is a volcano, the peak of which the grass of indecisiveness does not grow – Khalil Gibran

food recipes....*vyanjan, samagri, seedho and vidhi*

Sindh was the home to one of the oldest civilizations of the world, Indus Valley Civilization. Sindhi's had to leave Sindh, Pakistan in 1947 after the partition of India. Without a land of their own, they spread out all over the globe creating a name for themselves as great traders, business men, philanthropists and spiritual teachers. Known for its distinct flavors and rich aromas, Sindhi food is soul satisfying and nurturing. As I travelled and lived in various countries and continents, I adapted my recipes to assimilate locally grown herbs and ingredients. Hence these recipes are modified and simple versions; cooked intuitively without measuring. I encourage you to cook intuitively and rejoice in your culinary explorations.

vegetables – bhajiyun or subzian

sindhi besaranji kadhi

Chick Pea Curry

ingredients – *samagri* or *seedho*

1 cup chick pea flour or Besan
4 tablespoons ghee or oil of your choice
1/5 teaspoon asafetida or hing powder
½ teaspoon each mustard seeds, cumin seeds and fenugreek seeds
½ teaspoon each chili, turmeric, cumin and coriander powder
1 teaspoon fresh grated ginger
10 okras split lengthwise
1 cup each, cubed tomatoes, potatoes, lotus root, cauliflower
½ cup each, sliced green cluster beans or guar, carrots, moringa drumsticks
5 Kokums soaked in little water
1 tablespoon tamarind paste
2 tablespoons finely chopped cilantro or Hara Dhaniya
2 twigs curry leaves
8 to 10 cups water

method – *vidhi*

In a large thick bottomed sauce pan heat the ghee. Add asafetida powder, mustard, cumin and fenugreek seeds. As they begin to splutter add chick pea flour or besan and stir. Keep stirring it on medium flame until it turns golden brown and releases a sweet aroma. Add water and bring it to a quick boil, stirring continuously to avoid the formation of lumps. Add potatoes, carrots, green beans, moringa drumsticks and lotus roots. Lower the heat and keep stirring while it boils and thickens, about thirty to forty minutes or until the vegetable are tender. Add cauliflower, okras, tamarind paste, strained kokum, curry leaves, grated ginger, green chilies, and chopped cilantro. Continue boiling it for fifteen to twenty minutes, till all vegetables are well cooked in a thick curry like consistency. This tangy, tongue tickling, lip smacking curry is an all-time favorite of my family and friends.

Share your favorite recipe from your childhood which you enjoy cooking. How does it connect you with your elders?

sai bhaaji

split pea, mixed vegetable and spinach curry

ingredients – *samagri* or *seedho*

1 cup washed and soaked *chana dal* or split peas
1 bunch of spinach
½ bunch each amaranth and fresh fenugreek leaves
1 handful Chuuko if available
1 teaspoon finely chopped dill or *Suva* leaves
2 tablespoon finely chopped coriander, cilantro or hara dhaniya
1 cup each, chopped onions, tomatoes and potatoes
½ cup each, chopped green beans, carrots and squash
1 teaspoon each finely minced or grated ginger, garlic, green chilies
1 tablespoon tamarind paste
1 tablespoon ghee or organic oil of your choice
½ teaspoon each, red chili, cumin and coriander powder
1/6 teaspoon asafetida or hing powder
salt to taste
water as needed

method – *vidhi*

In a large thick bottomed pot, heat the ghee or oil. Add asafetida powder, garlic, ginger and green chili paste. Slowly add the chana dal or split peas. Combine all other vegetable including green leafy ones and add to the *chana dal* mix adding about one cup of water. Bring it to a boil and reduce the heat to medium temperature and stir often, adding more water as needed. Gradually add all the spices and tamarind paste and cook till vegetable are all tender and mushy. Once all the vegetables are cooked to a soft pulp, blend them with a rotary egg beater or a whisk. The texture should be thick and soupy.

You can also cook this in a pressure cooker, but check your cooking timings and instructions.

How do you cook your greens? Write down your favorite recipe of greens which you enjoy cooking.

vanganran jo bharto

barbeque eggplant

ingredients – *samagri* or *seedho*

2 large skinned, roasted or grilled eggplants
2 cups chopped onions
1 cup chopped tomatoes
1 cup diced raw green mangoes
1 tablespoon minced garlic
1 teaspoon grated ginger
1 teaspoon finely chopped green chilies
½ cup finely chopped cilantro, coriander or hara dhaniya
1 tablespoon organic ghee or oil of your choice
½ teaspoon each, cumin seeds, crushed red pepper, black pepper, cumin and coriander powder
1 teaspoon garam masala
salt to taste

method – *vidhi*

In a large thick bottomed saucepan, warm up ghee or oil, add to it cumin seeds. As it begins to splutter, add the ginger, garlic and green chilies. Add onions and tomatoes, cook on medium flame until soft and mushy. Slowly add eggplants and raw green mangoes, continue stirring till it is well mixed. Cover and cook for ten minutes on medium heat. Once tender and cooked, add all the dry spices and salt. Stir and cook for another few minute, mashing it with a potato masher until soft and pulpy. Top with sliced green chilies and coriander, serve hot.

In Caribbean this dish is popularly known as *Baingan Choka* and is made without raw green mangoes.

How do you barbeque your vegetables? Write down your experimentation with the process of barbequing different vegetables.

guaar patatan ji bhaaji

tangy cluster beans and potatoes

ingredients – *samagri* or *seedho*

1 lb. chopped cluster beans or *guaar*
2 peeled and cubed potatoes
1 finely chopped onion
1 chopped tomato
1 teaspoon fresh minced garlic
1 inch piece peeled and grated ginger
2 finely chopped green chilies
¼ cup finely chopped cilantro
1 teaspoon coriander powder
½ teaspoon each, powdered red chili, cumin, turmeric and amchur
1 tablespoon organic ghee or oil of your choice
salt to taste

method – *vidhi*

Steam *guaar* beans and keep them aside. In a thick bottomed sauce pan, heat the oil and sauté garlic, ginger, green chilies and onion. Add tomatoes and dry masalas and mix it well. Cook on medium flame and gradually add steamed guaar beans and cubed potatoes. Cover and cook until *guaar* beans are tender. Garnish with cilantro and serve warm.

You may substitute *guaar* beans with any other green beans of choice and potatoes with yam for more fiber.

Green beans are nutritious, how do you cook them? Today cook your favorite recipe of green beans and play with some different spices.

aur ji sat bhaaji

mustard tempered mixed vegetables

ingredients – *samagri* or *seedho*

1 cup each, cubed potatoes, carrots and squash
1 cup each, sliced green beans, sweet green pepper and lotus root
1 cup cauliflower sprigs
1 large pureed tomato
1 tablespoon chopped or grated ginger
1 teaspoon minced garlic
1 tablespoon chopped green chilies
2 tablespoons chopped cilantro for garnish
1 teaspoon each, coriander powder and mustard seeds
½ teaspoon each red chili, cumin and turmeric powder
15 curry leaves
2 tablespoons ghee or oil of your choice
3 tablespoon whole wheat flour mixed with one cup water
salt to taste

method – *vidhi*

In a thick bottomed saucepan, heat the ghee and fry garlic. Sauté potatoes, green beans, carrots and lotus root. Add salt, turmeric, ginger and green chilies and pureed tomatoes. Add enough water to cover the vegetables and allow it to boil on medium flame until vegetables are cooked. Add cauliflower and sweet peppers and simmer for 10 minutes on slow flame. Gently add the flour and water mixture, stirring frequently to avoid formation of lumps. Once the sauce is thickened, lower the flame and cover. In a separate frying pan, heat a little ghee and add to it mustard seeds and curry leaves.

Once the mustard seeds start spluttering, add it to the vegetables simmering in the sauce and stir. Garnish with cilantro and serve hot.

What are some traditional vegetable recipes in your family? How can you cook them differently? Write down your thoughts here.

bhugal phool patasha beah

Gorgon Nuts and Lotus Root Curry

ingredients – *samagri* or *seedho*

1 cup sliced parboiled lotus root or beah
1 cup soaked gorgon nuts or phool patasha
1 cup cubed potatoes
1 cup cubed eggplant
1 cup bhugal masalo
1/2 cup tamatan ji pat
1/4 cup sao masalo
2 tablespoon ghee or oil of your choice
1 teaspoon cumin seeds
1 teaspoon fennel seeds or saunf
½ teaspoon each, red chili, cumin, coriander and turmeric powder
10 curry leaves
water as needed for the gravy
sliced green chilies and cilantro leaves for garnish
salt to taste

method – *vidhi*

In a large thick bottomed saucepan, heat oil. Add cumin seeds and when they start spluttering, add lotus roots, potatoes and eggplants. Sauté the vegetables and slowly add the bhugal masalo and tamatan ji pat. Simmer the vegetables in the sauce on medium heat adding water if needed. Once vegetables are tender, add sao masalo, curry leaves, fennel seeds, dry spices and salt to taste. Bring it to a boil, lower the heat, drain and add the gorgon nuts and allow it to simmer in the thick gravy. You may also add parboiled moringa drumsticks to this medley of vegetables. Garnish with sliced green chilies and cilantro leaves.

Do you experiment with exotic vegetables? How have you done that in the past? Note your thoughts here.

dhingree or khumbiyoon mutter

mushrooms and green peas

ingredients – *samagri* or *seedho*

2 cups sliced or diced mushrooms
2 cups green peas
2 table spoon Bhugal Masalo
2 tablespoons Sao Masalo
2 tablespoon Tamatan ji Pat
2 tablespoon sour cream or whipped yoghurt
1 teaspoon cumin seeds
1 teaspoon of coriander powder
½ teaspoon each of red chili, cumin, black pepper powder and garam masala
2 tablespoon ghee or oil
cilantro leaves for garnish
water as needed
salt to taste

method – *vidhi*

Heat ghee in a large thick bottomed saucepan and fry the cumin seeds. Combine the *bhugal masalo, sao masalo and tamatan ji tat* and stir well; bring it to boil adding little water. Add all the dry spice powders except black pepper and garam masala and lower the heat. As the sauce thickens add the green peas, mixing it well. After peas are cooked add mushrooms and stir well cooking it on medium heat for a few minutes. Stir in the sour cream and remove from the heat, garnish with black pepper, garam masala and cilantro leaves.

Share your favorite mushroom recipe, how do you like to eat your nutritious mushrooms?

aisee turee

curried ridge gourd

ingredients – *samagri* or *seedho*

3 cups diced ridge gourd or turee
1 cup chopped onion
1 cup chopped tomatoes
1 teaspoon grated ginger
1 teaspoon minced green chilies
½ cup finely chopped cilantro
½ teaspoon each dry coriander, red chili, turmeric and cumin powder
1 tablespoon organic ghee or oil of your choice
salt to taste

method – *vidhi*

In a large thick bottomed saucepan, sauté the onion until translucent. Add ginger and green chilies, stirring in tomatoes and *turee*. Cook on high flame until all the vegetable are well cooked and mushy, for five to seven minutes. Add all the dry spices and salt to taste. Cover and simmer on low flame until water has evaporated. Mash with a potato masher until soft and pulpy. Serve warm with Phulko.

Have you tried cooking or eating various gourds? How do you like to cook them?

seyala gogroon

ginger garlic turnips

ingredients – *samagri* or *seedho*

1 lb. peeled and cubed turnips
1 cup chopped tomatoes
1 cup chopped onions
2 tablespoons sao masalo
1 teaspoon coriander powder
½ teaspoon each, powdered cumin, red pepper, turmeric and black pepper
¼ teaspoon garam masala
1 tablespoon organic ghee or oil of your choice
cilantro leaves for garnishing
salt to taste

method – *vidhi*

In a thick bottomed sauce pan, heat up the ghee or oil. Sauté the onions until they are golden translucent, add *Sao Masalo* and tomatoes. Cook on medium flame till the sauce is pulpy. Add turnips and all the dry spices, stir well. Cover and cook on low flame until the turnips are tender and well cooked. You may garnish it with cilantro leaves and garam masala if you wish.

How would you create a variation of this dish? Go ahead, experiment!

sukal masalan jyun bheendiyun

spicy sautéed okras

ingredients – *samagri* or *seedho*

1 lb. tender okras
1 tablespoon, organic ghee or an oil of your choice
2 tablespoon dry coriander powder
2 tablespoon red chili powder
1 teaspoon dry mango or amchur powder
1 teaspoon black pepper
1 teaspoon cumin powder
½ teaspoon turmeric powder
1 teaspoon salt

method – *vidhi*

Mix all the dry spices in a bowl and keep them aside. Wash, dry and slit the okras lengthwise; cutting the top and bottom. Stuff the dry spice masala into okras through the slit. Heat the ghee or oil in the shallow pan, coating the bottom thoroughly. Carefully arrange the masala stuffed okras in the pan. Gently cook okras on a slow flame, turning every few minutes until the okras are cooked evenly. Serve hot with Phulko or Mani. Sometimes to spice it further I add a tablespoon of Tamatan ji pat and sao masalo to the okras while they are being cooked.

Do you usually fry your okras? I love them fried too, but here is a healthier version. How would you cook it differently?

lentils – dalyun or dal

tidalee dal

three lentil and bean soup

ingredients – *samagri* or *seedho*

1 cup split peas or chana dal
¼ cup cracked green beans or split moong dal
¼ cup cracked black lentil or split urad dal
2 tablespoon organic ghee or oil of your choice
1 teaspoon coriander powder
½ teaspoon whole cumin seeds
½ teaspoon each, red chili, cumin and turmeric powder
¼ teaspoon asafetida or hing powder
2 tablespoons finely chopped cilantro
1 tablespoon tamarind paste
1 teaspoon minced garlic
1 teaspoon grated ginger
3 to 4 cups water
salt to taste

method – *vidhi*

I generally cook this dal in a slow cooker or a pressure cooker, depending on time. It can also be slow cooked in a thick bottomed saucepan. Wash all three dals and soak them for a few hours, rinse and drain the water. In a thick bottom vessel combine water and dal and bring to a rapid boil. Add turmeric and salt and cook it on medium flame, until lentils and beans are soft. Add grated ginger and tamarind paste, cover and let it simmer. Beat it with a rotary beater until dal is well blended and creamy. Heat the ghee or oil in a small frying pan, add cumin seed and asafetida. Slowly add garlic, green chilies and all dry spices. Add this mixture in the boiling dal and stir well.

You may substitute different lentils, legumes and beans in this soup. Garnish with cilantro and serve warm.

Do you enjoy soups? I love soups, have you incorporated lentils for protein in your soups instead of meat? Try it!

dal pakwan

a twofold recipe of spicy split peas with crispy bread

ingredients – *samagri* or *seedho* for *dal*

2 cups split peas
1 chopped tomato
4 finely chopped green chilies
2 tablespoons finely chopped cilantro
1 teaspoon grated ginger
1 teaspoon cumin seeds
1 teaspoon each, red chili, cumin, and coriander powder
½ teaspoon each of turmeric and dry mango or amchur powder
5 black peppercorns
2 tablespoons organic ghee or oil
3 cups water for cooking
salt to taste

method – *vidhi*

Wash and soak the dal and keep it aside for two hours. In a large thick bottomed saucepan, heat the ghee or oil. Add the cumin seeds, black peppercorns, ginger and green chilies, fry for a couple of minutes adding drained dal, salt, red chili, turmeric, coriander and cumin powder. Stir continuously while cooking on a medium flame. Add tomatoes and stir fry some more, gradually adding water and increasing the heat. Cover and bring it to a boil, lower the heat and allow it to simmer until split peas or dal is soft and tender. Garnish with dry mango powder and cilantro before serving with Pakwan.

dal pakwan - continued

ingredients – *samagri* or *seedho* for *pakwan*

2 cups white flour
1 teaspoon cumin seeds
2 teaspoons organic ghee
oil for frying
water for kneading the dough
salt to taste

method – *vidhi*

In a large mixing bowl, mix the flour with salt, cumin seed and oil. Add water gradually, kneading the dough to a medium pliable consistency. It should neither be stiff or too soft. Divide the dough into six portions, dust the rolling surface with flour and roll out six inch circles. Prick the surface with a fork and deep fry each Pakwan at a time in hot oil. Serve hot with dal and sundh ain gidamari ji chatreen.

Do you have any family recipes that involve two different methods of cooking? Write down your thoughts.

breads – mani or roti

phulko or mani

unleavened flat bread

ingredients – samagri or seedho

2 cups organic whole wheat flour
salt to taste
water to knead the dough
2 tablespoons organic ghee or oil of your choice

method – vidhi

Keeping aside the ghee, combine the ingredients into a large bowl. Add water slowly kneading it into firm but pliant dough. The more you knead the dough, the softer your roti. Cover the dough and preferably set aside for twenty minutes. Divide it into ten to twelve small balls. On a well dusted rolling board, roll each ball into a thin four inch circle with a rolling pin. Heat a flat griddle and roast this roti, chapatti, Phulko or Mani, turning it over until it is well cooked and small golden brown specks appear on the surface and it puffs up. Apply a touch of ghee and remove from heat.

Your favorite bread recipe and why do you love it? Share it here.

mitho lolo

sweet crisp bread

ingredients – *samagri* or *seedho*

2 cups organic whole wheat flour
½ cup organic brown sugar or ground jaggery
½ cup ghee
1 cup water to boil the sugar or jaggery
5 crushed green cardamoms or elaichi
water for kneading the dough

method – *vidhi*

In a large saucepan mix the water and sugar or jaggery, bring it to a slow boil on medium flame. Stir it well till the sugar or jaggery is dissolved and the syrup is of medium consistency. Remove it from the stove and strain it strain it into another clean bowl and allow it to cool. Next mix the whole wheat flour, green cardamoms, ghee and pour the syrup into it slowly, mixing it gently and kneading the dough to a stiff consistency. If needed you may add a little water while kneading the dough. Divide it into four balls and roll these out in thick circles. Pierce gently with a fork so it is well cooked inside. Bake or roast these on a girdle or *tava*, turning and cooking it on both sides. Apply ghee or oil while roasting as needed for a more crumbly, flaky texture. If baked thick it is popular during festivities as *Mitho Lolo* and if baked thin it is known as *Mithi Loli*.

How do you add sweetness to your breads? Have you experimented with various sweeteners like agave and honey? Pen your thoughts here.

koki, loli ain besanreen

savory crisp bread

ingredients – *samagri* or *seedho*

3 cups organic whole wheat flour
2 finely chopped onions
4 finely chopped green chilies
1 tablespoon crushed pomegranate seeds or anardana
2 tablespoons cilantro, coriander or Sava dhana leaves
7 tablespoons ghee
½ teaspoon fresh crushed black pepper
½ teaspoon red chili flakes
salt to taste
water to knead the dough

method – *vidhi*

Combine all the ingredients in a large mixing bowl, keeping aside two tablespoons of ghee for later use. Knead the mixture into stiff dough, mixing all the ingredients thoroughly. Divide the dough into eight portions and roll each portion into a small four to five inch thick circle and prick it with a fork, so it is well cooked. Roast it on a griddle or tava, turning and pressing it as it is roasted or baked properly. Apply ghee or oil as you see golden brown spots appear on the surface.

This bread can also be baked without onion and pomegranate seed, and dry roasted.

You may also substitute whole wheat flour for chick pea flour or *besan*, making it a b*esanreen*; another delectable bread.

Simple and tasty, these savory breads could be eaten plain, with pickles and chutneys or with other accompaniment dishes.

Do you spice up your breads? What herbs and spices would you like to experiment with? Write them down.

mooriyah payi mani

flat bread stuffed with radish

ingredients – *samagri* or *seedho*

2 cups organic whole wheat flour
3 tablespoons organic ghee or oil of your choice
1 grated Daikon or radish
2 tablespoons finely chopped cilantro, coriander or hara dhaniya
1 finely chopped green chili
½ teaspoon each, powdered red chili pepper, cumin, coriander and black pepper
salt to taste
water to knead the dough

method – *vidhi*

In a medium bowl combine grated radish, cilantro, green chili and all the dry spices. Keep aside for twenty minutes, squeeze out the juices and divide into eight portions. Keeping aside the ghee, combine the salt and flour in a large bowl. Add water slowly kneading it into firm but pliant dough. The more you knead the dough, the softer your roti. Cover the dough and preferably set aside for twenty minutes. Divide it into eight small balls. On a well dusted rolling board, roll each ball into a thick four inch circle with a rolling pin. Apply ghee and sprinkle flour, keep a portion of radish mix and wrap up the dough around the mix to form a little parcel. Dust with flour and gently roll it out into six inch circular flat bread. Heat a flat griddle and roast stuffed *mani*, turning it over until it is well cooked and small golden brown specks appear on the surface. Apply a touch of ghee on both sides, pressing with a spatula so it is well cooked. Once baked, remove from heat.

You may also stuff this *mani* or paratha with spicy boiled mashed potatoes, grated spicy carrots and even spicy boiled moong beans.

Do you stuff your breads with vegetables or infuse them with herbs and spices? Try doing that and watch what unfolds.

kareleji kaat payi mani

bitter gourd crisp flat bread

ingredients – *samagri* or *seedho*

3 cups organic whole wheat flour
½ cup *kareleji kaat* or grated, salted and dried bitter gourd
2 finely chopped onions
4 finely chopped green chilies
1 tablespoon crushed pomegranate seeds or anardana
2 tablespoons cilantro, coriander or dhaniya leaves
4 tablespoons grated, salted, sautéed bitter gourd or Karela skin
7 tablespoons ghee
½ teaspoon fresh crushed black pepper
½ teaspoon red chili flakes
salt to taste
water to knead the dough

method – *vidhi*

Sauté the grated salted and dried *kareleji kaat* or grated bitter gourd in a little ghee and set it aside to cool. Combine all the ingredients in a large mixing bowl, keeping aside two tablespoons of ghee for later use. Knead the mixture into stiff dough, mixing all the ingredients thoroughly. Divide the dough into eight portions and roll each portion into a small four to five inch thick circle and prick it with a fork, so it is well cooked. Roast it on a griddle or *tava*, turning and pressing it as it is roasted or baked properly. Apply ghee or oil as you see golden brown spots appear on the surface.

Karela can be substituted with grated *paneer, moong* bean sprouts, leftover sautéed *dal* or lentils and even leftover brown rice *pulao* or spicy *quinoa*.

Have you ever tried this vegetable? Try cooking a little differently today.

sindhi doli

leavened whole wheat puffed bread

ingredients – *samagri* or *seedho*

4 cups organic whole wheat flour
1 teaspoon organic brown sugar
1 teaspoon instant yeast
½ teaspoon fennel seeds
½ teaspoon Shahjeera seeds
½ teaspoon onion seeds
½ cup warm milk to knead the dough
oil to fry the bread
water to knead the dough
salt to taste

method – *vidhi*

In a bowl mix the whole wheat flour and dry ingredients. Knead the dough first with warm milk, gradually adding enough water to form pliable dough. Cover and let it rest until it doubles. Knead it thoroughly once again, divide it into small balls and set aside for some more time. When ready to fry, roll it with a rolling pin into small 4 inch discs. Deep fry in hot oil until it puffs up, turning it gently a couple of times. Remove from the fryer, onto the paper towel to remove excess oil. Serve hot with *Dhingree* or *Khumbiyoon Mutter*.

What would be an alternative method of cooking this bread? Should we bake it? What do you think?

dhodho

multi grain crisp bread

ingredients – *samagri* or *seedho*

2 cups millet, rice or sorghum flour
1 finely chopped onion
2 finely chopped green chilies
2 tablespoons finely chopped green garlic or chives
2 tablespoons finely chopped coriander, cilantro or Dhaniya leaves
2 tablespoons ghee
salt to taste
water to knead the dough

method – *vidhi*

Keeping aside ghee, combine all the ingredients in a large mixing bowl, adding water slowly to make stiff dough. Divide this dough into four or five ball. Pat these balls between your palms into a circular stiff pancake, if needed moisten your hands for spreading the dough. On a heated griddle or tava carefully transfer this pancake and cook it on medium flame. Turnover and cook on the other side, drizzling with a little ghee till crispy. Cook till well cooked on both the sides. Remove from griddle and serve with butter, ghee or yoghurt.

What are your thoughts on multi grain bread? Experiment today with different grains.

chillo

savory pancake

ingredients – *samagri* or *seedho*

2 cups organic whole wheat flour or chick pea flour
1 finely chopped onion
3 finely chopped green chilies
1 finely chopped tomato
1 tablespoon finely chopped coriander, cilantro or *dhaniya* leaves
1 tablespoon finely chopped mint or pudina leaves
¼ teaspoon chili lakes
¼ teaspoon turmeric powder
¼ teaspoon fresh crushed pepper
¼ teaspoon ajwain seeds
2 teaspoons ghee to drizzle
salt to taste

method – *vidhi*

Keeping aside ghee, combine all the ingredients in a large mixing bowl, adding water slowly to form a thick batter of pouring consistency. Heat a griddle or a shallow frying pan and pour about three to four tablespoons of the batter, spreading it quickly as you would a pancake. Cook on a medium flame for a couple of minutes and turn it over. When both the sides are cooked, drizzle a little ghee on the edges to make it crispy.

Have you tried a savory pancake before or savory crepes maybe? Play with your ingredients.

satpuro

crisp layered flat bread

ingredients – *samagri* or *seedho*

2 cups organic wheat flour or white flour
½ teaspoon of salt
½ teaspoon of fresh crushed coarse organic black pepper
¼ cup organic brown sugar
2 tablespoons ghee
organic oil of your choice for deep frying and kneading
water for kneading the dough
optional sliced pistachios and almonds for garnish

method – *vidhi*

In a large bowl mix the wheat flour, salt, black pepper, ghee and knead it into soft dough with adequate amount of water. Cover and keep it aside for an hour or two. Separate the dough into 4 or 5 portions. Roll each piece of dough into a thin circle. Cut it into two halves. Slice each half into thin strips about ¼ inches. Sprinkle these strips with flour and oil and roll them into small pinwheels. You should have two medium size pinwheels from each portion of dough. Roll these pinwheels into circular thin bread. You can now deep fry them in hot oil in a frying pan or you may alternately roast them on a griddle, turning them a couple of times and applying little oil until they are thoroughly cooked and are flaky and have golden flakes on them.

In India, fried *satpuro* is served as a sweet dish, sprinkled with brown sugar, dried rose petals, sliced pistachios and almonds. In the Caribbean they add a ¼ teaspoon of baking soda to the dough mix and it is cooked on a girdle and popular as BussUpShut Roti.

Would you like to cook it differently? Go ahead do it!

seyala mani

green garlic infused bread

ingredients – *samagri* or *seedho*

5 leftover mani, phulko or chapatti torn into small pieces
1 large chopped onion
1 large chopped tomato
2 tablespoons Sao Masalo
1 teaspoon each, mustard seeds and cumin seed
1 teaspoon coriander powder
½ teaspoon each red chili, cumin and black pepper powder
2 tablespoons finely chopped cilantro
1 teaspoon finely chopped green chilies
1 tablespoon lemon juice
10 curry leaves
3 tablespoons organic ghee or oil
water as needed
salt to taste

method – *vidhi*

In a large thick bottomed saucepan, heat the ghee or oil and fry mustard and cumin seeds. Stir in the chopped onions and cook until translucent. Add Sao Masalo, tomatoes, green chilies, coriander, red chili, cumin powder and salt. Mix well, add little water and bring it to boil. Lower the heat, add the leftover *mani* and curry leaves. Simmer on low flame until the sauce is absorbed by the *mani*. Garnish it with lemon juice and cilantro.

You may also substitute *mani* with bread slices, it tastes equally delicious.

I think left over brown rice would be a good substitute too, shall we try it?

rice – chanvaran or chawal

photey bhugal khichadi

cardamom flavored rice and lentils

ingredients – samagri or seedho

1 cup white or brown rice
¼ cup split moong beans or split green lentils
5 crushed cardamom pods
2 tablespoons organic ghee or oil
2 cups water
salt to taste

method – vidhi

Wash and soak rice and lentils, set aside for an hour. Heat the ghee or oil in a thick bottomed saucepan and sauté the crushed cardamom for a couple of minutes. Add the rice and lentil mix, salt and water. Stir well and bring it to a rapid boil on high flame. Cover and let it simmer over low flame until all the water has evaporated and rice, lentil mix is cooked. You may have to increase the time and quantity of water if you use brown rice. I normally use rice cooker while cooking the rice dishes as it keeps the rice warm until I am ready to serve it.

Quinoa and Farrow would be good too in this recipe, what do you think? Should we experiment?

sava chanvaran

savory golden rice

ingredients – *samagri* or *seedho*

2 cups white basmati rice
1 tablespoon grated ginger
1 tablespoon minced garlic
1 tablespoon finely chopped chives, green garlic or sai thuma
1 teaspoon finely chopped green dill or soova leaves
1 tablespoon organic ghee or oil
½ cup fresh green peas
½ teaspoon fine cumin, caraway or shahjeera seeds
½ teaspoon turmeric powder
1 large bay leaf
5 black peppercorns
4 cups water
salt to taste

method – *vidhi*

Wash and soak the rice and set it aside for an hour. In a thick bottomed saucepan, heat the ghee on medium flame and fry shahjeera, bay leaf and pepper corns. Add garlic, ginger, chives and dill leaves to the mix. As the garlic turns golden add, rice, green peas, salt and turmeric. Stir well and add water, bringing the mix to a rapid boil. Cover, lower the head and allow it to simmer until water is evaporated and rice and peas are cooked. Once again this can be easily cooked in a rice cooker and kept warm till you are ready to serve it.

How would you cook this differently?

bhugal chanvaran

aromatic brown ice

ingredients – *samagri* or *seedho*

2 cups white or brown basmati rice
1 sliced onion
1 cinnamon or dalchini stick
4 cloves
4 cardamoms
4 black peppercorns
1 bay leaf
½ teaspoon caraway or shahjeera seeds
2 tablespoons organic ghee or oil
4 cups water
salt to taste

method – *vidhi*

Wash and soak rice for an hour and keep it aside. Heat the ghee or oil in a large thick bottomed saucepan; fry the sliced onion until golden brown. Stir in cinnamon stick, cardamoms, black pepper corns, cloves and *shahjeera*. Drain the rice and add it to the mix in saucepan, stirring it properly. Add water and salt and bring it to rapid boil. Lower the flame and cover the saucepan. Let it simmer on low flame, until all the water is evaporated and rice is cooked. You may add mixed vegetables or soya chunks during the cooking process to make it into a hearty one pot meal, serving it with plain yoghurt, *raita or matho*.

Can you experiment with more grains? Which ones would you choose and why?

taahereen

festive sweet rice

ingredients – *samagri* or *seedho*

2 cups white or brown basmati rice
3 tablespoons organic ghee
6 cardamoms
½ teaspoon fennel seeds
1/3 cup organic brown sugar
1 tablespoon each, sliced almond and pistachios
1 tablespoon grated dry coconut or doongi
¼ cup raisins
3 cups water
a pinch of saffron
a pinch of salt

method – *vidhi*

Wash and soak rice and keep it aside for an hour. Heat ghee in a large thick bottomed saucepan, add cardamoms and drained rice. Stir fry rice for a few minutes; add water, saffron, fennel seeds and salt. Bring it to boil and cover and simmer till rice is half cooked. Add sugar and sprinkle a little more water if needed, mix well. Cover and allow it to simmer on low flame, until rice is cooked. Remove from heat, garnish with grated dry coconut, raisins, pistachios and almonds. This is usually served on festive occasions with *sai bhaaji* and b*hugal phool patasha and beah bhaaji.*

Should we play with agave nectar or organic maple syrup as a sweetener? What do you think? Experiment!

pickles and condiments
achaar, matho ain chatriyun

dudh or dahi

yoghurt

ingredients – *samagri* or *seedho*

2 cups whole milk
1 tablespoon yoghurt culture

method – *vidhi*

In a thick bottomed saucepan, bring the milk to a full boil. Pour it in an earthen or glass container and allow it to cool to about 110 degrees, it should be warm to touch. Add yoghurt culture and whisk it well. Leave it overnight undisturbed in the pantry or the oven, making sure that the oven is not turned on. It will be set by morning, move it into the refrigerator. For more creamy yoghurt, mix 1 cup half and half milk with 1 cup whole milk. This fresh yoghurt can be used in both food and skincare recipes.

Can you find a different recipe to make yoghurt? Write it down here.

swanjhre je gulan jo matho

moringa flower yoghurt

ingredients – *samagri* or *seedho*

2 cups whisked or whipped yoghurt
1 cup steamed Moringa flowers or Swanjhre ja Gula
1 teaspoon roasted cumin seed powder
¼ teaspoon each red chili, black pepper and coriander powder
1 table spoon each finely chopped mint and cilantro leaves
1 finely chopped green chili
pinch of black salt for additional flavor
salt to taste

method – *vidhi*

Squeeze out excess water from the steamed moringa flowers and keep them aside. In a large serving bowl mix all the ingredients except mint and cilantro leaves and roasted cumin powder. Add moringa flowers to yoghurt mix and whisk it well. Garnish with roasted cumin powder, mint leaves and cilantro. You may substitute moringa flowers with grated cucumbers, boiled corn, diced boiled potatoes, savory *boondi* or *sev*. It makes a great dip with Papad. Serve chilled!

How differently can you serve this?

sundh and gidamari ji chatreen

ginger and tamarind chutney

ingredients – *samagri* or *seedho*

2 cups tamarind pulp
1 cup pitted dates
1 teaspoon dried ginger powder or Sundh
1/4 cup organic brown cane sugar or powdered jaggery
1 teaspoon roasted cumin powder
salt and red pepper to taste

method – *vidhi*

Blend all the ingredients together in a blender. In a thick bottomed saucepan, bring the blended sauce to a boil on a medium heat, stirring frequently. Continue stirring the sauce till it thickens and forms a syrup consistency. Remove from heat, cool and store in an airtight container. May last for 15 days if stored refrigerated properly in fridge.

This may be used as a garnish on m*atho* or *raita* and diluted it also makes a great tangy tamarind salad dressing.

How about substituting or adding applesauce to this recipe? How do you think it would taste?

ambriyoon jyun bidryun

grated mango pickle

ingredients – *samagri* or *seedho*

4 cups salted grated raw mangoes
1 teaspoon dried ginger powder or Sundh
1 teaspoon each, fennel seeds, cumin seeds, onion seeds and peppercorns
1 tablespoon red chili powder
1 cinnamon stick or dalchini
3 bay leaves or kamaal pat
10 cloves of garlic
1 pinch nutmeg powder
1/4 cup organic brown cane sugar
1/2 cup cooking vinegar
2 cups mustard oil
salt to taste
unbleached muslin cloth cut into 2 X 2 inch pieces and a spool of unbleached thread

method – *vidhi*

Squeeze out the excess moisture from previously grated salted raw mangoes. In a large thick bottomed saucepan, mix all the ingredients except vinegar, oil, muslin cloth and spool of thread. Set it aside for an hour. Add half a cup of oil to the mix, then gently cook on a low flame and stir thoroughly. Once half cooked to a golden color, stir vinegar into the mix and remove from the flame and allow it to cool. On a small precut muslin square place a tablespoon of pickle mix and tie it into a little bundle with a piece of thread. Gently place these little bundles one by one in the glass jar. Once all the *bidris* or bundles are placed in jar, top it with remaining warm mustard oil and seal it airtight. Leave it out overnight but store it in refrigerator next day onwards for a longer shelf life. This recipe has been modified by me. Originally pickling was a slow process and the jar was left out in the sun for 21 days, occasionally shaken gently without opening. These pickles would then last for months without spoiling. When ready for your pickle scoop one *bidri* out of the jar, open it, discard the thread and muslin square and enjoy your pickle!

Do you think we can substitute with other vegetables? What would you substitute raw mangoes with?

dessert

kheerni

creamy rice pudding

ingredients – *samagri* or *seedho*

4 cups full cream milk
1 cup soft cooked rice
1 cup organic brown sugar
5 pods green cardamoms or elaichi
2 tablespoons each, sliced pistachios and almonds
2 tablespoons each, raisins and sliced dates
a pinch of saffron

method – *vidhi*

Bring the milk to a rapid boil on high flame, in a large thick bottomed saucepan. Reduce the heat to medium stirring it continuously for at least ten minutes making sure that it does not stick to the bottom. Add soft cooked rice, brown sugar and cardamoms. Lower the heat further and let it simmer till the milk thickens to the consistency of a soft creamy pudding. Add raisins, dates, saffron and mix well. Garnish with almonds and pistachios.

You may substitute rice with vermicelli, semolina, sago nuts, brown rice and even quinoa. This desert can be served warm or chilled.

Your favorite desert and why you love it? What is missing in our life that we need to add external sweeteners? Express your thoughts here.

chuurie or kuttie

whole wheat crumble

ingredients – *samagri* or *seedho*

1 cup organic whole wheat flour
¼ cup organic ghee
¼ cup organic brown cane sugar
unsalted raw peanuts, sliced dates, finely sliced coconut and fresh cut fruits are optional

method – *vidhi*

Melt the ghee in a thick bottomed saucepan. Add the whole wheat flour and stir fry until a sweet aroma emanates from it and it turns golden brown. Remove from heat and add brown cane sugar and stir the mixture until it resembles a crumbly texture. This is also served as an offering to various deities during fasting and spiritual gatherings. You may optionally add unsalted peanuts, sliced dates, finely sliced coconut and fresh cut fruits, before serving.

Chanting and praying while you cook it, will raise the vibration of the food.

Note here your favorite ceremonial sweet dish recipe. Why is it sacred to you?

atte jo seero

whole wheat offering

ingredients – *samagri* or *seedho*

1 cup organic ghee
1 cup organic whole wheat flour
1 cup organic brown cane sugar
5 crushed cardamoms
3 cups water

method – *vidhi*

Mix sugar and water and bring it to a boil in a saucepan. In a separate thick bottomed saucepan, melt ghee on a medium flame. Add whole wheat flour and crushed cardamoms to the melted ghee and stir fry until it releases a sweet aroma and turns golden brown, usually about fifteen minutes. Add sugar water syrup to the flour and ghee mixture and cover it, as it will start spluttering. Slowly open the lid and stir the mixture that begins to thicken on a slow flame. Keep stirring until it separates from the sides of the pan. Remove from flame and chant a prayer of gratitude before serving it warm.

Also known as *Karah Prasad* this is served during the Sikh prayer gatherings as *Prasad* or offering. Recite mool mantra, guru mantra or a prayer, while you cook it with love.

List any soul satisfying sacred offerings from your childhood memory that you love. How do you feel when you eat them? Does it evoke a sense of sacredness?

skincare recipes and treatments....*nuskhe aur upchaar*

Ayurveda has time-tested recipes for a glowing skin. You can have a soft, supple, clear and radiant skin without spending a fortune. There are ingredients in most kitchens which when used correctly can balance and beautify your complexion. A note of caution here, it is recommended that if you are trying to be pregnant, pregnant, lactating or menstruating; kindly consult with your aesthetician, Ayurvedic practitioner or healthcare provider before trying any new recipes or rituals. These skincare recipes are only for topical application and should not be ingested. Here are some of my favorite natural skin care recipes.

basil and almond eye tonic

ingredients – *samagri*

4 fresh basil leaves
4 fresh mint leaves
2 teaspoons almond oil
1 teaspoon honey

method – *vidhi*

Crush the mint and basil leaves and squeeze the juice. Mix it with almond oil and honey and whisk it. Apply gently under the eyes with your ring finger; as this exerts least pressure. This should be done before retiring to bed at night.

Write here another soothing eye cream recipe that you have read and found effective.

cilantro and mint aromatic mist

ingredients – *samagri*

1 cups distilled water
1/8 cup chopped cilantro
1/8 cup fresh chopped peppermint leaves
4 drops of organic peppermint essential oil

method – *vidhi*

In a small saucepan, bring the water to boil and remove from the heat. Add the fresh chopped herbs, cover and allow steeping for an hour. Add essential oil and stir well to blend the ingredients. Strain and store in a suitable pray bottle, close your eyes and spritz on your face or apply with cotton all over the face after cleansing. Should be refrigerated immediately after use and will last up to a week.

How does this make you feel? Close your eyes and allow your senses to enjoy these aromas.

uplifting orange mist

ingredients – *samagri*

8 ounces distilled water
4 drops of organic orange essential oil

method – *vidhi*

In a spray bottle or atomizer, mix well distilled water and essential oil. Closing your eyes spritz gently all over face, neck and décolleté as need. It can be stored for six months if refrigerated.

What other ingredients would you use to mist your face with and why?

purifying lemon mist

ingredients – *samagri*

4 cups distilled water

½ cup organic apple cider vinegar

15 drops of Lemon essential oil

method – *vidhi*

Combine ingredients in a large measuring cup, blend well. Pour into a spray bottle or an atomizer. Closing your eyes, spritz gently on face, neck and décolleté as needed. It can be stored for six months if refrigerated.

Does this revive any memories? What are the aromas telling you? Listen!

chick pea and lemon cleanser

ingredients – *samagri*

1 teaspoon chick pea powder
1 tablespoon freshly extracted lemon juice
A pinch of turmeric

method – *vidhi*

Mix all three ingredients in a bowl. Apply gently all over face in a circular motion, avoiding eye and lip area. Rinse off thoroughly. You may substitute milk or cream for a dryer skin.

How do you cleanse your skin? Would you like to try something different?

almond cleanser and exfoliant

ingredients – *samagri*

10 Almonds
¼ cup milk
A pinch of turmeric

method – *vidhi*

Overnight soak almonds in milk. When ready to use, blend it in a small blender adding a pinch of turmeric. Apply all over face, avoiding the eye and lip area. Rinse off with tepid water after a few minutes.

What can you substitute almonds with and why?

almond and licorice moisturizer

ingredients – *samagri*

1 tablespoon almond oil
1 teaspoon rosewater
1 teaspoon licorice root
1 teaspoon beeswax
3 teaspoons water

method – *vidhi*

Soak licorice root in three teaspoon water for five to six hours. In a heat proof glass bowl, mix the almond oil and beeswax. Place over a pan of boiling water and melt over low heat with a wooden spatula. Once melted, remove from heat and add licorice infusion; stirring until mixture cools and thickens. Store it in a clean sterilized jar. Refrigerate if needed.

Note down here your favorite moisturizers and why you like them. Do you think you can recreate them in your kitchen?

yogurt and fenugreek exfoliant

ingredients – *samagri*

1 tablespoon fresh organic yoghurt
3 teaspoon fenugreek seeds
a pinch of turmeric powder

method – *vidhi*

Overnight soak fenugreek seeds in yoghurt. When ready to use, blend it in a small blender adding a pinch of turmeric. Apply all over face avoiding the eye and the lip area. Leave it on skin for a few minutes, removing gently in circular motion. Rinse with tepid water and pat dry the skin.

What other ingredients do you think work well as a natural exfoliant without scratching the skin? Have you experimented with any exfoliating ingredients? Be gentle with your skin, nature knows how to exfoliate your skin, it just needs very little help from you. Choose your natural ingredients wisely and never over exfoliate.

creamy chick pea mask

ingredients – *samagri*

1 cup organic milk
4 tablespoon chick peas
1/8 teaspoon turmeric
10 drops lemon juice

method – *vidhi*

Soak the chick peas in the milk overnight. Blend it in blender adding the turmeric and lemon juice. Apply all over the face avoiding the eye and lip area. Rinse it off after ten to fifteen minutes. Discard left over mask. This is great mask for clarity of skin.

What are you covering with a mask? Are you unmasking your inner radiance? You are radiantly beautiful, embrace this truth.

orange and turmeric mask

ingredients – *samagri*

2 teaspoons chick pea powder
2 tablespoons milk
1 teaspoon dried orange powder
½ teaspoon turmeric powder

method – *vidhi*

Blend well all the ingredients in a blender or whisk them well with a rotary whisk. Apply on cleansed skin, avoiding the eye and lip area. Allow it set, remove with tepid water after fifteen minutes. Discard the left over mask. This is a great mask for skin prone to hyperpigmentation.

Your skin recognizes these ingredients as you have ingested it at some time or other. Your gut recognizes what you are applying on your skin and works effortlessly with these natural ingredients.

milky cucumber mask

ingredients – *samagri*

½ cup milk
½ cup grated cucumber
1 teaspoon rose water

method – *vidhi*

Blend well all the ingredients and apply all over the face, avoiding eye and lip area. Remove with tepid water after twenty minutes. A very runny mask, keep a wash cloth on hand to catch the crumbs. This mask has soothing and calming properties and can be used for all skin types.

What does the aroma of roses remind you of? Are the cucumbers cooling your skin?

lemon and arishtha shampoo

ingredients – *samagri*

2 cups dried soapwort or Arishtha nuts
2 tablespoon freshly squeezed lemon juice
water for soaking the nuts

method – *vidhi*

Overnight soak the *arishtha* nuts in two to three cups of water. In the morning gently boil the mix for fifteen to twenty minutes. Strain and allow to cool, adding the lemon juice. Shampoo your hair with it and rinse off with water.

Is your hair ready for some gentle cleansing? Try this recipe.

hibiscus and rose petal hair conditioner for dark hair

ingredients – *samagri*

1 cup rose petals
1 cup hibiscus petals
1 cup marigold petals
½ cup mint leaves
½ cup basil leaves
1 teaspoon organic ghee or coconut oil
2 to 3 tablespoons water

method – *vidhi*

In a small blender, blend all the above mentioned ingredients. Apply on shampooed hair, directly on your scalp. Leave it on for twenty to thirty minutes; wash off with warm water, followed by a cold water rinse.

Is your hair over processed? Is it looking for some nourishment? Here is a simple recipe for darker hair.

almond rose lip cream

ingredients – *samagri*

1 tablespoon organic almond oil
1 teaspoon rosewater
1 teaspoon honey

method – *vidhi*

Whisk all the above mentioned ingredients in a small bowl until creamy. Apply as needed to soften the lips. Store in a sterilized glass container, refrigerate if needed.

Are you lips smiling and praying today? Offer them some loving nourishment with this recipe.

mint and cinnamon toothpaste

ingredients – *samagri*

1 tablespoon of cinnamon powder
1 teaspoon of mint juice
1/8 teaspoon of black pepper
¼ teaspoon of mustard or sesame oil
a pinch of salt

method – *vidhi*

Mix all the above mentioned ingredients in a bowl. Apply this paste with your index finger, gently massaging your teeth and gums. You may also use a soft brush but be very gentle. Gargle and rinse off thoroughly.

Have you experimented with different teeth cleaning products? What do you like about them and why? Pen your thoughts here.

rose and sandalwood foot lotion

ingredients – *samagri*

1 cup coconut oil
¼ cup rosewater
1 teaspoon sandalwood essential oil

method – *vidhi*

In a small blender, blend the above mentioned ingredients until creamy. Store in a sterilized glass jar and use every night as you retire; make sure to wear clean cotton socks after application to avoid staining of bed linen.

They have carried you all your life, how do you express your gratitude to your feet?

rose and almond hand lotion

ingredients – *samagri*

1 tablespoon organic almond oil
2 tablespoon rosewater
1 teaspoon apple cider vinegar
1 cup organic honey

method – *vidhi*

In a small saucepan, gently warm up almond oil, rose water and apple cider vinegar. Add honey, turn off the heat and whisk the mixture until cool and creamy. Store it in a sterilized glass bottle and use frequently.

Namaste, as you join your hands in gratitude do you think about nourishing your hands?

conclusion....*nishkarsh*

I am convinced that the greatest legacy we can leave our children are happy memories: those precious moments so much like pebbles on the beach that are plucked from the white sand and placed in tiny boxes that lay undisturbed on tall shelves until one day they spill out and time repeat itself, with joy and sweet sadness, in the child now an adult
– Og Mandino

As I traversed the wide space of the memories of my childhood and youth, writing this homage to my grandmother Sugi, I looked at the faces of my beloved children. Now young adults, they have brought me immense joy, through the many lessons they have taught me. As we held each others' hands cruising through life, I realized that it was not I who was holding their hand as we navigated this canoe of daily existence through the stream of life; they were the anchors balancing my canoe. As a parent, I always wanted the best for them and so I realized that the best way was to be transparent and lead them by example.

Leading them by example meant being totally authentic, allowing them to see my vulnerable side as well as my stronger side. They were privy to all the information as I healed my body. They travelled with me to the various meditation and yoga retreats and self-improvement classes which I took.

While our daughter shopped with us as we visited various farmers markets learning to make healthy choices, our son helped us grow our organic kitchen garden. Our son-in-law brought his own sense of awareness with him and was always eager to share his knowledge and to imbibe our perspective.

As Sandeep and I raised our children, we came to the realization that while a parents role is to nurture their children as they grow, it is also true that children give their parents a reason to dive deep and bring out their own best, so both can flourish.

As I look back fondly at our journey together, I realize that if we each take care of our own family unit, there would be more peace on this earth. It all begins in the nurturing environment of our own home. The care and love that goes in cooking at home, translates into happy and healthy children. The love we nourish our children with, translates into responsible citizens. As we take care of our own home, we also help create a better environment for ourselves and our neighbors. Above all as we take care of our self, we set examples for our children and others and allow them the opportunity to do the same. Nurturing others can truly be accomplished, if we learn to love and nurture our self. I have never seen an empty vessel fill another empty vessel, have you?

Gathering together the flowers of over one hundred and eight recipes and rituals for radiance, I offer my children, my teachers and my readers this bouquet of opportunity to stroll through their inner garden. True radiance is possible only when your mind, body and soul are in balance. I chose the path of Ayurveda to connect with my ancestors and heal my body through the lessons learned from them. I encourage you to return to your own roots and dig into the soil of your soul, for many stories will then be revealed to you in the form of: branches of beauty, leaves of legacy, fruits of faithfulness and seeds of spirit.

Sow these seeds into the fertile soul of your child's mind and leave a legacy of love and nourishing practices.

Design your week by picking seven recipes from each category. On my fridge I have a magnetic weekly erasable calendar with seven columns, one for each day. On Sunday I organize myself and mark my calendar. For each day I pick a positive word, a skin or body care recipe and a food recipe. Each day, I meditate or reflect on the chosen positive word, what it means to me, what memories does it evoke, how has it strengthened me in the past and how can I apply it in my life now to bring more joy? I pick seven self-care recipes, that will help me to indulge in the pleasure of the aromas, touch and arouse in myself a moment of self-love and self-appreciation. Then

I pick seven recipes for food; plan my menu, shop for the organic ingredients. I cook with joy and eat it peacefully with pleasure, savoring each bite, chewing consciously and delighting in various tastes hidden in every morsel. As I nourish myself, I nourish the divine within myself. I invite you to do the same.

At the altar of our own divinity, let us offer *akshat* or some grains of our spirit, *pushp* or the fragrant flowers of our thoughts, *dhoop* or the incense of our intellect and light the *diya* or a bright lamp of our knowledge. Let us all love one another and let us all glow!

Asato Ma Sat Gamaya, Tamaso Ma Jyotir Gamaya, Mrutyor Ma Amrutam Gamaya
– Bhadranayaka Upanishad

Lead me from the untruth to the truth, Lead me from the darkness to light, Lead me from the death to immortality
– Bhadranayaka Upanishad

To my children with love....

*Deep within my being
Was an abscess
Nothing
Could fill
You knew I was lonely
You knew I was sad
You entered in my womb
And asked me to just wait

I yearned for your arrival
So I could hardly wait
God listened to my prayers
And brought you
In my arms
A little early than late

My joy knew no bounds
As He said
You have asked for too little
And as he added
Once again
To my half - filled cup
He blessed me over twice

You both have been
A blessing
You have been
My source of joy
On dark nights
When I was sinking
Your tiny arms
Lifted me high*

My love for you
Is endless
God's grace has
Overflowed
When I think of
His countless blessings,
I couldn't have asked for more

glossary....*shabdhkosh*

Aarti – Hindu worship ritual
Abhaar – Acknowledgement, Gratitude
Abhaar – Gratitude
Abhyanga – Full body massage
Abhyanga – Massage
Achaar – Pickle
Acharan rasayana – Science of positive thoughts and conduct
Adar – Respect
Adhbhuta – Wonder
Adhmiyakta – Spirituality
Adrak – Ginger
Aisee turee – Ridge guard
Ambriyoon jyun bidryun – Grated mango pickle
Anardana – Pomegranate seeds
Anghooti – Ring
Anukampa – Kindness
Arishtha – Soap nuts
Attar – Perfume
Atte jo seero – Whole wheat offering
Aur ji sat bhaaji – Custard tempered vegetables
Ayur – Life
Ayurveda – Science of life
Badam – Almonds
Bazaars – Market place
Beah – Lotus root
Besan – Chick pea powder or flour
Besanreen – Savory Indian bread
Bhajiyun – Vegetables
Bhakti – Devotion

Bhaya – Fear
Bhugal chanvaran – Aromatic brown rice
Bhumika – Introduction
Bichua – Toe ring
Chakra – Energy center
Chakra – Energy Centers, Spirals
Champi – Scalp massage
Chand Raat – New Moon
Chandan – Sandalwood
Chandra – Moon
Chanvaran – Rice
Charaka Samhita – Ayurvedic text written my Charaka
Chawal – Rice
Chillo – Savory pancake
Choka – Indo-Caribbean cuisine
Chooriyan – Bangles
Chuurie – Whole wheat crumble
Dahlpuri – Indo-Caribbean cuisine
Dal – Pulses and lentils
Dal pakwan – Two fold meal of lentils and Indian crisp bread
Dalchini – Cinnamon
Dalyun – Pulses and lentils
Dargah – Islamic shrine
Darshan – Visitation
Devi – Goddess
Dhairya – Patience
Dhaniya – Cilantro
Dhatu – Metal
Dhingree – Dehydrated minced mushrooms
Dhodho – Multigrain crisp bread
Dhrrta – Perseverance
Dhyaan – Meditation

Dincharaya – Daily routine
Diwali – Indian festival of light
Doli – Leavened bread
Dosha – Body constitution type
Doubles – Indo-Caribbean cuisine
Durga – Goddess
Dushala – Stole, Scarf, Shawl
Elaichi – Cardamoms
Gajra – Floral garland for adorning the hair
Gandoosha – Oral oil pulling
Ganesha – Remover of obstacles
Garam Masala – Allspice, mixture of spices
Ghee – Clarified butter
Gogroon – Turnips
Granthasuchi – Bibliography
Guaar patatan ji bhaaji – Cluster beans and potatoes
Gurudwara – Sikh temple
Gurumukhi – Punjabi script
Haar – Necklace
Haldi – Turmeric
Hasya – Joy
Henna – Herbal dye
Hersh – Joy
Itihaas – History
Jeera – Cumin
Jhulelal – Deity of the sea
Kachri – Dehydrated wafers
Kajal – Kohl
Kalari – Martial art from Kerala
Kalari – Martial arts
Kamar Patti – Ornamental waist band
Kansa Vataki – Tri metal bowl

Kapha – Combination of earth and water
Karah Prasad – Whole wheat sacred offering
Kareleji kaat payi mani – Indian bread stuffed with grated bitter gourd
Karn phool – Earrings
Karna Purti – Ear oil massage
Karuna – Compassion
Kaya kalpa – Transforming therapy
Kheerni – Creamy rice pudding
Khumbiyoon – Fresh mushrooms
Koki – Savory Indian bread
Kshipra – Quick, River, Pulsating, Flowing
Kum Kum – Red powdered adornment on the forehead
Kundalini yoga – A yoga practice taught by Yogi Bhajan and his teachers
Kuttie – Whole wheat crumble
Lahsun – Garlic
Lavang – Cloves
Loli – Savory Indian bread
Maina – Myna
Mala – Garland
Mangal sutra – Auspicious onyx or coral bead necklace
Mantra – Vedic Chants
Mantras – Spiritual chants
Marma – Vital energy centers
Marma Chikitsa – Manipulation of vital energy centers during a massage
Matha Patti – Head adornment
Mehndi – Henna
Mirch – Red pepper
Mool mantra – First verse from Sikh scripture
Moong dal – Green pulses

Mooriyah payi mani – Indian bread stuffed with radish
Mudras – Hand gestures
Mukunda Upanishad – Hindu spiritual text
Naada – Music
Nadi – Channels of energy, energy pathways
Namaste – Greetings, Salutations
Nath – Nose ring
Nava Rasa – Nine essences
Neem – Azadirachta indica
Neti – Cleansing of nasal passages
Netra Basti – Soothing eye wash
Nishkarsh – Conclusion
Nrithya – Dance
Nuskha – Recipe, Remedy
Padabhyanga – Foot massage
Padagaatha – Massage by feet
Panchabhutas – Five elements
Panchakarma – Fivefold cleansing and rejuvenating program
Papad – Dehydrated lentil crackers
Parmananda – Bliss
Pavitrata – Purity
Payal – Anklets
Philourie – Indo-Caribbean cuisine
Phool patasha – Gorgon nuts
Photey bhugal khichadi – Cardamom flavored rice and lentil
Pishinchali – Vigorous full body massage
Pista – Pistachios
Pita – Combination of air & fire
Prakriti – Nature, Constitution
Prana – Energy
Pranayama – Breathing technique
Prashthabhumi – Background

Prathana – Prayer
Prema – Love
Pudina – Mint
Purva karma – Series of oil massages before Panchakarma
Pushpa – Flowers
Radha – Beloved of Krishna
Ragas – Notes
Ramayana – Hindu scripture
Ramcharitmanas – Hindu scripture
Rattan – Gems
Ritucharya – Seasonal routine
Roti – Indian unleavened bread
Rudra – Anger
Saadar Pranam – Respectful greetings
Sai bhaaji – Greens
Samagri – Ingredients
Santosh – Contentment
Satai – Sindhi festival
Satchidanand – True heartfelt bliss
Satpuro – Seven layered crisp bread
Satvikta – Purity
Sava chanvaran – Golden rice
Seedho – Ingredients
Seyala mani – Garlic and mint infused bread
Shabdhkosh – Glossary
Shahjeera – Fine cumin
Shanta – Peace
Shiroabhyanga – Scalp massage
Shirodhara – Deep relaxation Ayurvedic therapy
Shishu abhyanga – Infant massage
Shringara – Adornment
Sigri – Coal burning stove

Sika – Affection
Sindhi – People of Sindh origin or ancestry
Sindoor – Vermilion powder
Sneha – Affection
Soothika abhyanga – Post natal massage
Subzian – Vegetables
Sukal masalan jyun bheendiyun – Spicy sautéed okras
Sundh ain gidamari ji chatreen – Ginger and tamarind chutney
Suva – Dill
Swanjhre je gulan jo matho – Moringa flower yoghurt
Taahereen – Festive sweet rice
Talahridaya – Heart center, Heart beat
Thadri – Sindhi festival
Tidalee dal – Three pulses and lentils
Tridoshic – Well balanced dosha
Tulsi – Basil
Ubtan – Cleanser and exfoliator
Ubtan – Local application of powder or paste
Ulhas – Happy
Upchaar – Treatment, therapy
Vanganran jo Bharto – Barbeque or roasted eggplant
Vata – Combination of space & air
Veda – Knowledge
Veera – Courage
Vibhatsa – Disgust
Vidhi – Method
Vinamrata – Humility
Vishaysuchi – Table of contents
Vishesh – Deep tissue massage
Yoga – Yoked or union

bibliography....*granthsuchi*

Books that have inspired me on this journey....

Chopra, Deepak. *Ageless Body, Timeless Mind,* New York, Crown, 1993.

Chopra, Deepak. *Creating Health,* Boston, Houghton Mifflin Company, 1987.

Chopra, Deepak. *Quantum Healing,* New York, Bantam Books, 1989.

Chopra, Deepak. *Perfect Health,* New York, Crown, 1991.

Douillard, John, Dr. *The Encyclopedia of Ayurvedic Massage,* Berkley, North Atlantic Books, 2004.

Frawley, David. *Ayurvedic Healing,* Salt Lake City, Passage Press, 1989.

Johari, Harish. *Dhanwantri,* New Delhi, Rupa Publications, 1992.

Lad, Vasant, and David, Frawley. *The Yoga of Herbs,* Santa Fe, Lotus Press 1986.

Lad, Vasant, *Ayurveda: The Science of Self-Healing,* Wisconsin, Lotus Press, 1984.

Miller, Light, ND & Miller, Bryan, DC. *Ayurveda & Aromatherapy,* Wisconsin, Lotus Press, 1995.

Rosenthal, Joshua. *Integrative Nutrition®: feed your hunger for health and happiness,* Austin, Greenleaf Book Group LLC, 2011.

Sachs, Melanie. *Ayurvedic Beauty Care,* Wisconsin, Lotus Press, 1994.

Sachs, Melanie and Robert. *Ayurvedic Spa,* Wisconsin, Lotus Press, 2007.

Svoboda, Robert E. *Ayurveda: Life, Health and Longevity,* Arkana, Penguin Books, 1992.

Tiwari, Maya. *Ayurveda, A Life of Balance,* Vermont, Healing Press, 1994.

Tiwari, Maya. *Secrets of Healing,* Wisconsin, Lotus Press, 1995.

Websites explored on my journey into wellness….

Chopra, Deepak Dr. www.chopra.com
Douillard, John Dr. www.lifespa.com
Hay, Louise. www.hayhouse.com
Lad, Vasant Dr.www.ayurveda.com
Rosenthal, Joshua. www.IntegrativeNutrition.com
Sachs, Melanie & Robert. www.DiamondWayAyurveda.com
Tiwari, Maya. www.mayatiwari.com
Google Search engines. www.google.com

About the Author

Pratibha Masand Sachdev MA, Bombay University, lives in Houston, Texas with her family and enjoys creating organic food and skincare recipes for radiance. An International skincare educator, she is also experienced in product research and development. A voracious reader and writer, she loves penning her thoughts as much as learning from other authors. A licensed aesthetician with over eighteen years of experience, she holds prestigious CIDESCO diploma. Trained in various holistic modalities including Reiki, Reflexology, EFT, Yoga, Aromatherapy and Ayurveda, she is a Certified Holistic Health Coach; accredited by the American Association of Drugless Practitioners.

You can visit her online at: letiglow108.com

Made in the USA
Lexington, KY
07 March 2015